KU-515-127

RICHARD
HAMMOND'S
CAR CONFIDENTIAL

RICHARD
HAMMOND'S
CAR CONFIDENTIAL

Richard Hammond and Andy Wilman

WEIDENFELD & NICOLSON

Being a Modern Motorist

Contents

1

The Knowledge

Introduction

Motoring touches our lives in so, so many ways: driving a car, driving a car slowly (or quickly), being driven in a car, watching a car being driven, standing near a car as it drives past – the list is endless. And since I spend so much of my life describing; driving; crashing; collecting; prodding; tinkering with; stuffing the dog, wife and kids into; and, very occasionally, kicking cars I think I know the subject quite well.

My previous book, *What Not To Drive*, tackled, in the main, the issue of which cars are cool and uncool, pinpointing which ones you can be proud to be seen in and which ones require the driver to wear a paper bag over the head whilst out and about. In this new book, pearls of wisdom – essential nuggets of advice you cannot buy for love nor money elsewhere – continue to tumble forth, but across a much broader range, as I look at the whole issue of being a modern motorist. For example, just what are the worst motoring crimes? They're not the ones you might think. And what are you supposed to think of other road users such as bus drivers and cyclists? In case you don't know, I've got your opinion already written out for you in a nice handy section. Is it okay to do a dodgy customising job on your car in polite society? You may think not, but your pikey endeavours have extremely aristocratic roots. And what car should you have as a hearse? I know people usually have other things on their mind when they're dying, but it's surprising how little thought is given to the car you'll take your last journey in. On a more cheery note, I've also taken the liberty of revolutionising the world of in-car games for long journeys. Mine are so much better than the ones in coloured boxes in the shops.

All of the above, and more, comes in the first part of the book, the advice section. The second part is dedicated to wonderful, wonderful car trivia – not the gnomey stuff that car bores trot out in real-ale pubs, but a distillation of truly colourful gems that will interest even the most hardened Green. We look at the most embarrassing car in history, the wildest cars that never got made, the best car stunts, the most insane motoring laws around the world and the biggest motoring disasters and failures – and much, much more. There's loads of good stuff in here. Think of *Car Confidential* as an old friend. And also as a reasonably priced present for an old friend…

Being A Modern Motorist

The
Spotter's Guide
TO MODERN MOTORISTS

First of all, you've got to know what you're going to come up against out on the roads. At one time you could have relied on the class system – tradesmen drove vans and toffs drove Rolls-Royces – but these days, with BMWs outselling Fords, angry chefs driving around in Bentleys, Madonna in a Mini and Jade Goody in a Porsche, the roads are a much more egalitarian and confusing place. For this reason I have created the Spotter's Guide to Modern Motorists. Now, the Spotter's Guide has defended our shores more than once. Back in World Wars I and II, there were Spotter's Guides posted on every street corner, featuring silhouettes of military aircraft seen from below, basically so that Tommy knew what Jerry was throwing at him that day. In fact, if it wasn't for the Spotter's Guide, we might today be speaking German and shopping our neighbours for mowing their lawns on even-numbered Wednesdays.

So, here is the updated version for the new millennium. Obviously you're unlikely to encounter a Messerschmitt ME109, guns blazing as it spits a hail of red-hot death from its wings, but you could be on the tail of an ASBO about to spit a hail of red-hot litter from his stolen Rover. So I recommend that you keep this chart with you at all times. The obvious thing to do would be to cut out the warning figures and paste them to the inside of your windscreen or mount them on a spring in the glove box, where you'd normally keep a comedy boxing glove to surprise hitchhikers. However, both these methods could impair your vision, so instead I suggest you paste them to the back of a sun visor. It could mean the difference between life and a great deal of inconvenience.

Unmarked Copper A tricky one this, but with some Poirot-level scrutiny, you'll spot the telltale signs – the indentation from the hat brim on his hair cut, the outline of the tank top, and the speedo at 71 mph all lead to the inescapable conclusion that you're behind an officer of the law. The only evasive action is to put your foot down and do 72.

Weekend Shopper These people are the hidden menace of the road. They only take the car out on the Sabbath, and then it's only to buy stuff from warehouses they've seen advertised on the telly. Consequently they're unfamiliar with their cars so they have no idea what won't fit in them. Also, because they only ever turn off dual carriageways into shopping centre car parks, they have no idea how to drive. Be prepared for them to make sudden manoeuvres to chase after buses because they've spotted an ad for a closing-down sale on the back.

Environmentalist Steam – real red-hot, centre-of-the-earth steam – will be coming out of her ears, partly because of all the cars on the road and partly because she has to use her car to get to the Ban The Car meeting, which is miles away in a lay-by in Wiltshire. Her rear vision will be impaired thanks to the patchwork of stickers for worthy causes, and she may be in a bit of a trance due to the side effects of the Tibetan air freshener.

Dogger Have we got this right?

Vet Easily mistaken, in silhouette, for a children's entertainer. The difference is in the erratic nature of the driving. If he [or she] is all over the road, it probably will be a vet, and that won't be a glove puppet stuck on the end of his arm.

Sales Rep These days Baroness Thatcher may be as mad as a barrel of bees, but there are plenty of young thrusters who still heed her words that any man over the age of 25 who finds himself on a bus is a numpty. Consequently they're out there, bombing up and down the motorways, and they're busy – too bloody busy. The car cockpit is a blizzard of multi-tasking, lap-dancing vouchers and hot trouserpress action, so let them storm ahead while you ease off the throttle and slip on an eight-track of Neil Kinnock speeches.

Old Biffer Used to be easily recognizable simply because he'd always be in a Rover, but the invasion of cheap Korean cars has muddied the waters. Telltale signs include nasal hair converging with ear hair – and that is a deaf aid, not an iPod. Whatever you do, don't follow him: he's bound to be headed the wrong way down a motorway slip road, or has set off to the corner shop for some cat food and is now embarking on a two-year journey to Cape Town.

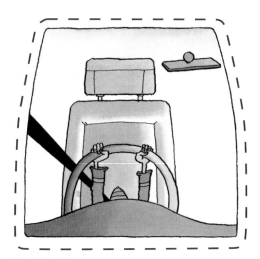

The Krankies You never know when this may come in useful.

Deal with Other Road Users

It'd be nice to live in a land where the only things you ever saw on the road were Lamborghinis and lollipop ladies, but sadly it's not so... Here's a run-down on the people you have to share the tarmac with.

CYCLISTS

Cyclists always seem to be angry. Now I've thought about this and the reason they're cross is not the fact that they get splashed by cars, or that they're using a form of transport that falls over when it stops. No, the anger wells up much earlier than that – when they get dressed. I'm talking here of course of the hardcore cyclists with the skin tight lycra and the melon shaped hard hat. They secretly know it's all wrong when they put the stuff on. I mean, there are other folk around who wear specific clothing to go from A to B, but they all seem to do carry it off with aplomb. Pilots for example, look pretty good, and frogmen are fairly cool. Cyclists though? I'm sorry, but no. I think the main problem is that the skin tight lycra, quite apart from the huge sweat patches radiating from the armpit and crotch areas, is all a trifle unnecessary. You're only going to work, for God's sake. Do you really need a hat with aerodynamic properties and Lance Armstrong's wardrobe for that simple journey? And when you get to work, and you're standing in the lift with a big sweat patch round your crotch, everyone will think you're a courier anyway. The Queen of England can do whatever she likes but she's never been seen in banana yellow lycra, so follow her lead. That's what she's there for.

BUSES

The zenith of our relationship with buses and bus drivers was in the early seventies. Back then, the bus was a big friendly thing, a bit like a pet elephant, and it either made you laugh because *On The Buses* happened to be on the telly, or it amazed you, like when *Blue Peter* showed a Routemaster going nuts on a skid pan. The Routemaster itself was an amazing vehicle, with aircraft-engineering design principles worthy of any science lesson. More than that, I genuinely believe that the Department of Buses at that time secretly had scriptwriters from Benny Hill or Dick Emery on the payroll. Every bus scenario had a comedy outcome: make the entrance to the bus an open bit at the back, because it'll encourage people to run after it, and if they've got shopping or they're drunk it'll be really funny. Also, give the conductor a machine that spits out a stream of tickets at the wrong moment, and a huge change bag that spews its contents everywhere when he chases fare dodgers.

Spool forwards to today, though, and the laughter has gone. Whereas bus drivers and motorists used to divvy up the road space between themselves, it's now done by the bus lane. This hateful invention couldn't have been bettered by Stalin: cordon off half the road and make it the privileged fast track for the few, except in our case the few aren't Politburo members, but pensioners off to get some tinned salmon and lottery tickets.

Then you have the buses themselves. No conductor, no manners, just one surly bloke behind a bullet-proof screen who thinks he's in the Queen's motorcade because some vegetarian lefty has given him his own lane. And now the situation is a whole heap worse thanks to the ginormous bendy buses that have already hit London and will no doubt be rolling out nationwide shortly. This could only be the work of an idiot like Ken Livingstone, who's never driven a car. "Right, we're one of the great capital cities of the world, how can we make it better? I know, introduce the sort of public transport they have in Cuba, where people use coconuts for shoes." To Ken, the bendy bus seems like a work of genius, but all that's actually happened is that bus drivers who didn't used to be hated by motorists, but now are because of their bus lane, and who used to be able to integrate with traffic, but have now lost the skill because of their bus lane, have been given a vehicle twice the size of the one they couldn't drive anyway.

The only way to reinstate harmony with the bus fraternity is to turn back the clock. Bring back conductors, Routemasters and Brylcreem for the drivers. Rip up the bus lanes and let bus drivers and motorists commune naturally. There'll be a few crashes at first, but, trust me, we'll sort ourselves out.

CARAVANNERS AND HORSE-BOX DRIVERS

I've put these two together because they share one big, important, annoying trait: their unparalleled ability to hold everyone else up just by going about their business. Viewers of *Top Gear* may remember – the caravan community certainly does – that we tried caravanning on the show one summer. As it turned out we had a car crash, reversed into everyone else's awnings and then burnt the site to the ground. So, frankly, it didn't go well, and the caravan world was pretty cross with us, but what sticks in my mind most is not the complaints from caravanners, but the feeling of hot sweat on the back of my neck as I looked in the extended wing mirrors at the gargantuan queue of suffering motorists snaking along behind us.

The question is how to solve the traffic problem and keep everyone happy. One solution would be for caravans to have plumbing and electricity that's already connected to the national grid, and be made of, say, bricks, and be a bit bigger, and have their own gardens. I don't know, you could call them houses or something, and then they wouldn't have to go anywhere. But caravanners do like to see new horizons, and new lace museums, so that wouldn't work. You could try fitting jet turbo and superchargers to the towing car, but most caravan drivers are 758 years old, and I think that would be an unwise marriage. In surveys, most motorists annoyed by caravanners believe they should only be allowed to travel at night, but I think that's a bit mean-spirited, frankly. No, I think the best idea would be to relocate all the caravanners to one place. You could move everyone out of, say, the Isle of Wight, or, if that's too much, Dungeness, and relocate the whole caravan community there. You'd call it Caravan Island and it would be like a huge safari park for caravanners and they could tootle about from place to place and only hold each other up. It could even provide a public service, because instead of giving ordinary motorists points for driving offences, you could send them to Caravan Island for a week, give them a really sexy sports car, and their punishment would involve having to run errands around Caravan Island at peak times.

Horse Boxes are a bugger. It's a pain for other motorists that some 20 year old girl with freckles and a bedroom full of rosettes is at the helm of a knackered Volvo towing a horsebox and a ton of horse. But you don't want her riding the horse to wherever she needs to go, because that way she'd be even slower and there'd be shit everywhere. Now inevitably she'll be on her way to a gymkhana, and this being the modern age, maybe you could solve the problem by having live web-cam-interactive gymkhanas. Basically, instead of everyone lugging their horseboxes at 23 mph to a field somewhere, all the competitors could stay put, do all the jumping and stuff in their own paddocks, and relay the pictures to each other via web-cams. The trouble is, though, gymkhanas and the like are the backbone of the rural community, and I like all that Countryside Alliance stuff, so it's important they get together. No, the only answer is two horses. You have a horse at home that you can groom and love and feed sugar lumps to, and another one, preferably cloned or, if not, at least painted with the same markings, already at the place where the event is. Simple.

BIKERS

I like bikers. They might annoy you by darting about and making a noise, and their fashion sense might be a bit dodgy, and they don't make good stand-up comedians, and they smell, and they generate one too many boring public-information films for my liking, but they're never guilty of the worst crime – holding you up. Also, unlike cyclists, they're never bitter when they see a nice car go by. And they are responsible for laudable things like keeping independent roadside caffs open, good pub juke-boxes, and Ginsters' profits. People get scared of their Hell's Angel image, but in truth the worst damage a biker can inflict on a car driver is the headshake. This is what happens when you're in slow moving traffic and your car is over to the right a bit too much, stopping the biker from squeezing through. And when he finally does get past, you'll see the biker shake his head in disgust. It's a small thing, but that slight motion of the helmet is utterly crushing. It says: "You can't drive, you have a tiny penis, your job is worthless, you contribute nothing to humanity, and what is more, I can't be bothered to turn round to tell you this."

The other issue to be aware of is the possibility of a biker coming to take your daughter out. I mean, honestly, bikes these days can do 200 mph, and they're cheap second-hand. Do you want your daughter, at the peak of her "He's a bastard and hasn't rung, I love him" phase, delivered into the bike world? So how do you stop this from happening? When the biker approaches, you could make your point by dousing his bike in petrol and then shooting his fuel tank with a shotgun, but a far more dignified and cheaper way of repelling bikers is to buy one of those door mats with "Please Wipe Your Feet" written on it. This to a biker is like garlic to a vampire. Your threshold will never be crossed.

Pass Your Driving Test

Now you've read the previous pages, you know who and what you're going to come up against on the road and you're pretty much ready to get out there and join them. There's just one final obstacle between you and the beginning of your life as a modern motorist: the driving exam – or more precisely, the driving examiner. While he may be a figure of fun, let's not forget that the driving examiner, despite the beige slacks, holds the key to your motoring freedom. So, once again, it's a case of finding out what you're up against. The only problem is that this time, it's much, much more tricky. Think about it: when did you last meet a driving examiner? Where do they go? Can you remember anything one has ever said to you? Do you remember their face? There must be thousands of them out there. So, where are they all? They're like the Men in Black, only they're the Men in Beige.

Let's examine what we actually know about them. They're incredibly secretive, they like driving and they're good at it. There's also something of the performer about them: think of the flamboyance with which they hit the dashboard for the emergency stop test – it's clearly the best bit of their day. And that moment at the end of ordeal: "I can tell you, Mr Smith, that you have…" then there's the enormous pause, building the tension before delivering the verdict of pass or fail – it's pure stagecraft. Clearly, this was a moment that had a big impact on a young Chris Tarrant, who later adopted the technique to great effect in *Who Wants To Be A Millionnaire?*.

The Faceless Characteristics Of An Examiner
Where are they and did office cleaners steal their formula for anonymity?

You are now in my powers and the events that take place over the next twenty to twenty five minutes will be erased from your memory. It is due to my lack of personality that I ended up doing this job and as it turns out it is the most perfect job for someone such as myself. My mum is still very proud of me however and she tells me so every day when I get home for tea. You are now in my powers and the events that take place over the next twenty to twenty five minutes will be erased from your memory. It is due to my lack of personality that I ended up doing this job and as it turns out it is the most perfect job for someone such as myself. My mum is still very proud of me however and she tells me so every day when I get home for tea. You are now in my powers and the events that take place over the next twenty to twenty five minutes will be erased from your memory. It is due to my lack of personality that I ended up doing this job and as it turns out it is the most

The Wacky Tie
Just to suggest that perhaps more lies beneath the beigeness.

The Ball Pen
Is it bic or X-men?

The Clip-Board
Is he collecting data on the human race and beaming it back to the planet they come from?

Non-Crease Fabrics
Also avaliable in beige.

Even if things get a bit tricky on your test, try to remain calm and confident. Remember, driving examiners spend their lives in hiding, so they will not react well to sudden movements or loud noises. Unless it's the emergency stop test, which they love.

Take the time to memorise *The Highway Code.* This is the only book your examiner will have read and enjoyed – many, many times. Turning round and saying "I dunno" when they ask you about it is like saying to a bishop that you thought the Bible was boring.

Wear a large signet ring with a mysterious symbol on it – I think it's probable that driving examiners are Freemasons, and Freemasons wear signet rings. So this might help, possibly.

Don't worry too much about rules: before joining the witness protection programme, your examiner was a getaway driver in a previous life – and probably did more than a spot of speeding in his time. Treat the speed limits more as a friendly guide.

THE HIGHWAY DRESS CODE

What you wear for your driving test is important. It sets the tone for the exam and can have a big effect on your confidence – and the examiner's mood. So, to give yourself a sporting chance of passing first time, try not to turn up wearing any of the following:

POLE-DANCER COSTUME While your confidence is to be applauded, it's sadly misguided. Unless your examiner is Benny Hill (unlikely, he's dead), you will probably only make them nervous, which will not help your cause.

FORMULA 1 DRIVER'S RACING OVERALLS The examiner is unlikely to believe you are a world-class driver who never got round to taking their test. And anyway, good as you may be, it's likely your driving ability will give you away fairly quickly.

Follow these simple guidelines and remember not to bump into anything or run anyone over on the big day, and you should be in with a chance of passing first time. Obviously, we cannot be held responsible for your failure to pass, or any incidences that arise from following these guidelines. Good luck and see you on the other side as a modern motorist.

WEDDING DRESS
Claiming your car driver has collapsed with a heart attack and the only way for you to get to your wedding on time is to pass your test and drive yourself straight there in the driving school's Nissan Micra is ingenious, but not entirely plausible.

MILKMAN'S UNIFORM Plenty of people need a driving licence for their job. Unfortunately, though, being a milkman does not entitle you to any special leniency on your driving test. The same goes for dropping your minicab driver's pass on the way across the car park or making claims about how the money you will earn driving a bus will pay for your grandmother's operation.

WHY
Customising
IS GOOD

If you're young and you've just passed your test, the first thing you'll probably do when you get your own car is crash it. Once it's mended, the second thing you'll do is customise it. Now, as a father of two with a house with a mantelpiece in Wiltshire, I'm supposed to be a bit sniffy about this. I'm supposed to scoff at Novas with big exhausts, but I absolutely love it. I adore seeing every badly fitted wing, every rubbish paint job, every over-ambitious front spoiler, every wildly optimistic turbo badge fitted on a 1-litre Saxo... Customising is an utterly joyful rite of passage in your motoring life when you express your individuality in the same way as you crack open the black paint and model your bedroom on a serial killer's den. It shows you have a pulse, you love life, you love your car. It also shows you can laugh at yourself. The guy with the Starsky and Hutch 2CV doesn't really think he's a pair of tough, over-cardiganned New York cops, and the person in the Renault 5 probably can't afford a Martini, shaken or stirred. Likewise, the kids in Japan aren't really expecting those wings and spoilers to get them recruited by talent scouts from McLaren and Ferrari.

"Lights... spoilers... and action!"

Often we get older viewers of *Top Gear* asking, "Why don't you have a laugh at those silly modded cars?" No, sod off! We'd actually rather snigger at your Porsche cufflinks. In fact, not only do I defend the right to carry out dodgy facelifts on your car, I'm still doing it myself. My pride and joy is this Land Rover, which has under-floor lighting and bass speakers so powerful they've caused the local cows to stop producing milk. Andy's caption for the picture above was "Richard Hasselhoff launches the new special edition Land Rover Baywatch." I can't think why.

Obviously the peak of customising these days can be found on the blinged-up cars of big R&B stars in America. Wyclef has a full-size fish tank in his Hummer, 50 Cent is chroming the entire bodywork of his Murcielago and now there are million-dollar-a-set, diamond encrusted wheels out there to tempt someone with a No. 1 album. But these chaps aren't the ultimate blingsters, and nor are they first. No, that honour goes to the Maharajas of India.

The Maharajas who ruled each State were fabulously wealthy and when they latched onto the existence of Rolls-Royce, Daimler and other high class makes, boy, did they go for it. In the early 20th century, the Maharajahs had on average more than three Rolls-Royces apiece, but the number wasn't the amazing part: it was the lengths they went to in blinging them up. The first Rolls to go out to India ended up with solid gold mountings and was owned by Prince Nizam of Hyderabad, but it was only one of the fifty Rolls-Royces in his garage, and all of them had V5s. Each Maharajah would fiercely try to outbling the other, adorning their cars with ivory steering wheels, panelling inlaid with diamonds, individually carved mascots and body panels fashioned from silver. And they weren't just for show: these bling-mobiles would often be seen thundering through the bush on tiger hunts, sporting huge, front-mounted spot-lamps for night hunting.

The Maharajahs knew they were Rolls-Royce's best customers, and woe betide any salesman who forgot that. One particular Indian noble, the Maharajah Kishan Singh, strolled into Rolls-Royce's London showrooms on one of his visits to the capital but was snubbed by sales staff because he was wearing dowdy clothing. So, how did he deal with his complaint? Did he ring the customer care line and listen to piped music for two hours? No, he did not. Instead, he returned to India and let Rolls-Royce know he would be converting three of their cars in his collection into rubbish-collection trucks.

Sometimes the famed quality of the Rolls-Royce engineering negated the point of the car's blingness. One Maharajah in southern India actually gave up driving his blinged Rolls and instead used an old clattery car for his journeys. Asked why, he complained that the Rolls ran too silently, giving his subjects no warning that he was coming and thus no time to pay homage. Ultimately, though, when it comes to all matters bling, the Maharajahs of India were untouchable and indeed in their home country they were only out-blinged once, a feat pulled off by Robert Matthewson, an eccentric millionaire living in Calcutta, who raised the bling bar to the stratosphere with the Swan Car in 1910. It cost him £15,000 at the time, and the body was carved from wood and plaster and finished in gold leaf. Then Matthewson's eccentricity kicked in, and the car was fitted with an organ and keyboard from which he could belt out tunes through the horn. The swan's beak was also designed to spray out hot water to clear the crowds away in the Calcutta streets, and fake bird poo was dumped out of the rear end as he went. Matthewson's amazing car made just one appearance on the streets of Calcutta before being banned by the police.

Deal with Dealers

Let's just think about modern motoring for a moment. The car is one of the most advanced engineering creations around. It has computers that see through fog, more computers that tell it not to crash into the car in front, and even more computers that measure a driver's eyelid movement and warn him not to nod off. Then there's the car industry itself. Over the course of the 20th century it's created the amazing art form of modern advertizing, put mass production on the map, helped invent the phenomenon of the teenager, and most important of all, given us crazy golf.

Now think about driving. Every day, hundreds of millions of us climb into machines that weigh two tons, and drive them at 80 mph within a few metres of each other. Thousands of cars come at us, again just a few metres away, from the opposite direction, and yet somehow it all works. Driving is one of the most amazing unrehearsed yet beautifully choreographed ballets mankind has ever performed. The act itself is a fantastic display of trust between strangers, a wonderful measure of civilisation evolving. Yes there are crashes, but in the main we pull it off, and we're not fighter pilots, just ordinary pot-bellied people going about our business.

Honest – it's a great little runner that the chicks will love!

But, sadly, wandering through this world of cutting-edge technology and Desmond Morris evolution is a big, backward, galumphing Troll. You can spot him by the Christmas cracker tie pin, the Harry Fenton suit and the bucket of hair gel that's been dropped onto his head by one of those planes that puts out forest fires. And certainly you'll find him in his natural habitat – the dealership.

Yes, despite all the advances in motoring, the dealer, and indeed the whole process of car buying that he presides over, is still in the dark ages. Put it this way: if you walk into Harrods and announce you're going to spend, say, £25,000, Al Fayed himself will carry you round the store in a sedan chair and floss your teeth as you go. Yet go into a dealership with the same spending intentions, and you'll be left on a bad chair next to a dead plant by the service desk, trying to avoid the dazzle from the dealer's Wayne Rooney commemorative cufflinks.

THE MODERN DEALER

Today, the quality of second hand cars is just that much better, meaning there's less call for the Dick Dastardly tricks. The mindset of the dealer, though, remains unchanged. When you walk into the showroom you are still an opponent to be upstaged rather than a customer to be wooed, and all that's happened is that the tricks have become a little more sophisticated.

It's no surprise that things are so grim really, because if you look back in history, the dealer family tree is decidedly iffy. In the post-war years a shortage of cars meant the whole business of car trading never got off to a fair start. Your loveable, trustworthy warm-hands local doctor was the biggest culprit, on account of the fact that medicine men were given priority over normal car buyers, and found they could run a tidy sideline shifting cars in between treating rickets and the plague. Then the motorist fell into the hands of the bunting-and-Portakabin traders, who exploited the technical ignorance of, well, everybody, in order to flog them mechanical dross. You had to hand it to them, these Arthur Daleys could find a good home for any mongrel. Want a diesel Merc? Sadly, Arthur has only got a petrol one, but once he's glued a 'D' badge on the rear end, you'll be none the wiser – and you'll be many miles away by the time you make your first fill-up. And have you ever wondered why so many traders queued up for pairs of tights in Boots? No, they're not Eddie Izzard. The thing is, hosiery works wonders at killing crunching noises when dropped into a knackered gearbox.

THE KEY SWITCH

Naturally, the dealer will be interested in your current car and will ask for the keys so he can give it a once-over. But the well-trained salesman will stick your keys in his office when he returns. If you want to go, you now have to ask for your key back – and the polite British don't like doing that.

KEEP IN POCKET AT ALL TIMES ▶

THE COFFEE TRAP

Some dealers will immediately offer you a cup of coffee. You welcome this hospitable gesture. But the canny ones will make sure it comes with powdered, rather than fresh, milk. This means the boiling hot coffee takes ages to drink, and the dealer has you captive for the next ten minutes.

THE TEST DRIVE

Now it's time for the test drive. The dealer will take you on a route he's planned out, and you can bet it'll involve plenty of right turns. This is because right turns require more concentration than left ones, and just as you're looking both ways, he'll fire in the questions: "What do you think of the car?..."

THE SOLUTION

The best way to deal with dealers is to be honest with them. Most people go into a showroom thinking that if they play their cards close to their chest, and pretend they're not interested in buying, they'll have the dealer on his knees. Nonsense. All this'll do is unleash his barrage of sales psychological warfare. If, however, you walk in and announce "I'm interested in buying today, but I'll be wanting your best price," everything should be rather more civilised.

Driving Games

Modern technology has done much to enhance road safety, speed up communication and cure diseases. But sadly it has broken up the family unit along the way. Happy family groups that once would have gathered round the mangle to watch the Queen are now scattered to distant corners of the house with their Game Boys, iPods, mobile phones and Gran Turismos. Thanks to modern technology, a new breed of child has huge over-developed thumbs, semi-transluscent skin the colour of cod and pink-rimmed, moon-sized eyes that glow in the dark.

Until recently, the family car journey was the last opportunity for the family to be together and communicate by means other than text. But even this is now under threat, thanks to the availability of in-car DVD systems for the price of a stamp. However, there's one last chance to use the car to keep the family bond alive and prevent your children from becoming crack addicts, car thieves and beggars or, worse still, IT consultants. Play my collection of technology-free in-car entertainment games and bring some old-fashioned, Waltons family values back into your life.

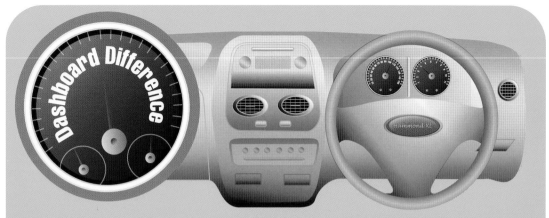

Suitable for: two players aged 8–80 • **You will need:** a dashboard • **Where to play:** best for passing time in a service station or supermarket car park, with the engine switched off.

How to Play

A game of 'spot the difference' skill. Each player takes it in turns to adjust the controls on the dashboard while the other one looks away. The other player then turns around and has twenty seconds to spot what has been altered. If successful, he takes over as 'Tweaker' while his opponent becomes the 'Spotter'. Should he fail, he plays again as 'Spotter' until successful. The game continues until Player 1 or Player 2 becomes bored and leaves.

Example of Play

Player 1 starts as 'Spotter' and looks away while Player 2, the 'Tweaker', moves the air conditioning control to the de-mist setting. Player 1 is given twenty seconds to spot this, but does so almost immediately. He takes over as 'Tweaker' and while his opponent – now the 'Spotter' – looks away, moves the indicator stalk to the left turn position. Player 2 fails to spot this in the allotted twenty seconds and once more must play as 'Spotter'.

Tips

Best played with the car stationary and switched off, partly because to do otherwise could be quite dangerous, but also because otherwise the operation of certain controls, such as seat heaters and radio volume, can easily be guessed at while looking away.

If playing with the engine switched on, you will have to bear in mind the sounds and visible effects of making certain changes – like, for example, flicking the indicators on – but skilled players will be able to find plenty of other tweaks to fool opponents. You might consider altering the fan setting by a single notch or changing one of the more obsucre settings on the stereo.

As an extra twist, why not try awarding extra points to players spotting the 'tweaks' quickly – perhaps giving 5 points if spotted within 5 seconds, 2 within 10 and just 1 point if it takes up to 20 seconds to spot the difference.

SEE THAT, THAT'S YOUR...

SUITABLE FOR: 2 PLAYERS AGED 8–80 • YOU WILL NEED: SOME EYES, SOME THINGS TO LOOK AT • WHERE TO PLAY: ANYWHERE THERE ARE THINGS TO LOOK AT

HOW TO PLAY

A game of visual and verbal skill. Each player must spot a particularly nasty example of something, such as, say, a house, and then attribute it to the other player thus: "See that, that's your house, that is." Upon seeing a rather run-down grocer's shop, the other player might then respond by saying, "You see that, that's the shop where you buy your groceries." It's important that once someone has been 'given' a particular item, such as a house, they cannot be given another. Play continues until an argument develops.

EXAMPLE OF A TYPICAL ROUND

Player 1 spies a rusty old car on bricks by the side of the road and 'gives' it to his opponent, saying, "See that, that's your car that is." Undeterred, Player 2 spots a very old and mildewed boat protruding from under a green tarpaulin. "You see that," he cries, "that's your boat and you're going to use it to sail over there to your marina," pointing to a duck pond with an up-turned trolley in it. "You see that," breathes Player 1, clearly moving in for the kill, "that is your best friend turning up outside your favourite petrol station on your motorbike to have an affair with your wife and use your mobile phone," and he points to a teenage thug cycling up to a disused petrol forecourt on a broken BMX bike to pet a mangy pit-bull terrier before urinating in a telephone box. A fight happens, the game ends.

TIPS

Multiple plays, such as the one detailed in the example above, are quite tricky to master at first. The beginner would best practice their skills with simpler, single plays such as "See that, that's your pet rabbit" when presented with an item of road kill.

When it comes to this game, the more colourful it is, the better. Quite often, a single imaginative play such as "You see that, that's your dressing-up box" when spotting a skip full old dog blankets can win the day, beating off the most elaborate and complex of multi-level plays.

See that, that's your fitness instructor, that is.

See that, that's your financial adviser, that is.

Longest
Finger in the World

Suitable for: 2–4 players aged 26

You will need: a car aerial(see note below) and a dashboard

Where to play: best in heavy or stationary traffic
as must be played from the back seat

How to Play

A game of dexterity and aerial-handling skill. Each player takes it in turn to use the aerial, or 'long finger' as it is called in the game, to carry out challenges nominated by their opponent. These challenges often increase in severity and difficulty as the match continues until it ends when a challenge cannot be met. The loser forfeits by having to refit the aerial.

Example of Play

Player 1 is challenged to pull down the passenger sun-visor using the 'long finger'. They achieve this and in turn, challenge Player 2 to open the driver's air vent and angle it to the right. This challenge is successfully met and Player 2 challenges Player 1 to re-tune the radio to Magic FM, adjust the air conditioning to 23.5 degrees and lock the doors. The game ends here.

Tips

For a more advanced version, you might try introducing time limits and penalties to the game. Under no circumstances should 'long finger' challenges include driving the vehicle on a public highway or operating any of the major controls while moving as this could be quite dangerous.

Note: the aerial can usually be unscrewed from the car roof. If in doubt, check the owner's manual. If the aerial is integrated into the windscreen, do not be an idiot and remove the windscreen.

SHAG 5

HOW TO PLAY

A game of lechery and sexist skill: start the game in a place frequented by people. Players must then choose from the next five members of the opposite sex they see from the car, the one they wish to, er, nominate. However, it's essential that each time they reject a potential candidate they cannot go back on that decision. If, therefore, they end up on No. 4 having not made their choice, they must accept No. 5, whatever they turn out to be.

This game works for women as well as men as there are plenty of examples of both to be seen on the streets. In fact, a game of mixed doubles can be most revealing and even exhilarating.

EXAMPLE OF PLAY

Let's take a mixed singles match between a man and a woman. The male first rejects a rather elegant young mother pushing an expensive buggy towards a taxi rank. His female opponent rejects a large man carrying a piano on his head, a drunken scaffolder and a cyclist with a skin disorder in quick succession. The male player discounts a matronly lady loading a tea chest full of vices into a Volvo then suddenly announces that he has chosen a sturdy but comely blonde in her mid-thirties, carrying a briefcase. Possibly she is an estate agent. The female player then rejects a well-toned but dismally ugly body builder. She has

now rejected four candidates and must accept the fifth, whatever happens. Meanwhile, the male player, having chosen the plump but pretty estate agent, now spots a leggy Elle Macpherson lookalike wearing a tool belt and carrying a book of poetry probably of her own writing, but is prevented from choosing again by the rules of Shag 5. He is dejected, and becomes even more so when the female player squeals with delight as Brad Pitt, on a rare trip to Burnley, turns the corner on his way to a visit to a local orphanage and catches her eye. Little does he know that he is her fifth and obligatory choice — game over!

TIPS

An alternative version of the game — possibly of European origin — exists where players agree on limits of play before commencing. Quite often it's the distance between two sets of lights, although the distance from where the car is located to the end of the next road will serve just as well in an emergency. Players are then given free rein to choose from any, or all potential — er — targets until the limit of play is reached. Again, it's essential that having elected not to choose a particular candidate, the player can not go back on his or her decision.

It's best to keep loud noises, pointing and expressions of disgust as discreet as possible, so as not to cause offence.

SHORTER GAMES FOR SHORTER TRIPS

All of the previous games are suited to longer spells in the car but even the briefest opportunity to spend time at play should be grasped and exploited. With that in mind, I have crafted the following selection of shorter games more suited to a visit to the shops than a trip to the coast.

PETROL STATION ROULETTE

Allow the car to run low on fuel to the point where the warning light comes on. Now see how many petrol stations you can pass with the light still on.

TREASURE HUNT

See who is best at spotting a pre-prepared list of 'treasure' items on the road:

- A Ferrari actually being driven fast (pretty rare – maybe save that for a longer trip)

- A 4x4 with mud on it (even rarer – wait for the summer holiday)

- A young person driving a Saxo without the front fog light on (rarer still)

THE COUNTING GAME

One for budding young mathematicians, see who can spot the most...

- TVRs on the back of AA trucks

- Vectras with jackets on hangers in the back window (actually an entirely separate game called Spot the Rep)

- MPVs going flat out in the fast lane driven by resentful dads who are not allowed a proper car (apart from the one you're in, of course)

THE FIRST TO SPOT

See who's fastest on the button and hits the target with the first...

- 50 Porsche Boxsters
  (ideal for a short journey to the shops)

- VW Phaeton or Renault Avantime
  (this could take a lifetime)

BMW LEAPFROG

Overtake a BMW and see how long the driver's ego takes to send them powering past again. Often lasts only a few seconds, so works well on shorter trips.

TRAFFIC COP CRICKET

The rules are similar to real cricket, only different. For every speed camera you pass on your side of the road, you score a run. A mobile speed trap is 4 and a camera flashing the car in front is 6. LBW is a camera flashing your car and if you spot a real-life traffic cop, you're out immediately. A camera going the other way is a run for the other side. An innings ends when ten cameras have been passed regardless of the weather, unless one of them was flashing a car opposite you when you were scoring a point. See, just like real cricket.

"Are we nearly there yet?"

Driving Clothes

What began as a physical necessity to protect passengers' pale Edwardian hides from the brutal elements has grown into a horror too terrible to contemplate in the 21st century. This is the story of driving clothes: from practical oilskin cloak to silk Ferrari blouson in a few misguided decades.

The Edwardians invented the car, but they never really got round to inventing the car roof – or window. Instead, they adopted a more direct approach to protecting passengers from the weather: swaddling them in layers of clothing so dense it was sometimes impossible to dig them out when they reached their destination. The illustration below shows how these early automotive pioneers unwittingly provided the inspiration for the Eewoks in *Star Wars*.

Big Floppy Edwardian Driving Hat

While his employers would stump up for the outer carcass of the big floppy hat, it was the responsibility of the chauffeur himself to provide the essential furry lining. By tradition as well as financial necessity, he would use road kill. Most drivers favoured badger or fox, but a hardy few made do with hedgehog (far more numerous in those days) or frog (unspeakably foul-smelling but with excellent waterproofing qualities). After a few years of being jerked about all over the road in pursuit of a particularly cosy-looking cat or weasel, the toffs decreed it was illegal for a chauffeur to kill an animal and wear it as a hat. Instead he must leave it for the next driver to come along behind him. As cars were quite rare back then, it might be some days or even weeks before another chauffeur happened upon the maggot-riddled results of a colleague's mishap with an animal, which they could turn into a lining for their hat. This may explain why car owners were not inclined to invite their chauffeurs to join them in sharing a fully enclosed car body.

Leather Driving Gauntlets

Early driving gauntlets – not, as you might think, the precursor to the more modern string-back driving glove, but actually the inspiration for those huge sponge hands popular at football matches – were precious items. In much the same way as a barrel-maker or cooper would be inaugurated into his trade by being rolled around in a barrel and beaten senseless, a young chauffeur would mark the completion of his apprenticeship by being taken to a dairy farm to be fitted for his driving gauntlets while they were still mooing. He would be marched by his seniors behind the ranks of cows in the milking shed and the cow that fitted each hand best would be selected. When he died, a chauffeur would always be buried with his gauntlets, largely because no one else fitted or wanted them and they often smelled quite bad.

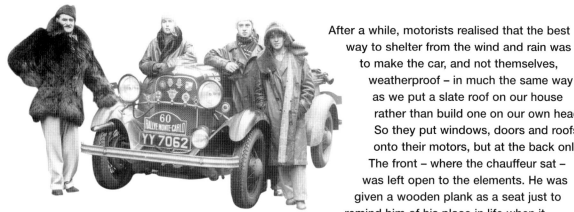

In their heyday, driving garments – whether big hats, furry coats or gloves so big you could keep your lunch in them – were as essential as the engine. They protected you from the elements and made you look raffish and sporty. Well, for the time, anyway.

After a while, motorists realised that the best way to shelter from the wind and rain was to make the car, and not themselves, weatherproof – in much the same way as we put a slate roof on our house rather than build one on our own head. So they put windows, doors and roofs onto their motors, but at the back only. The front – where the chauffeur sat – was left open to the elements. He was given a wooden plank as a seat just to remind him of his place in life when it stopped snowing. This is why an early chauffeur can be seen wearing a full-length leather coat with sixteen-inch high collars and leather gauntlets like failed veterinary experiments as he sits shivering on his wet plank while behind him his passengers loaf around in buttoned leather comfort wearing bikinis and togas, eating fruit and playing twister – cars were much bigger back then.

The sixties and seventies marked a low point for British fashion in general, and the driving clothes wadrobe must shoulder a fair share of the blame. In this era a chap only had Peter Wyngarde or The Persuaders to use as role models, which inevitably meant cravats, blousons and slacks were the order of the day, all woven from the finest man-made fibres in variations of Allegro beige. Today, though, order has been restored and driving clothes are much more tasteful, as the chap on the right demonstrates.

The Worst Car Crimes

The law would have you believe that the worst motoring crimes are offences such as car-theft and ram raiding. This is nonsense. Car theft is just someone expressing appreciation of your wheels, and ram raiding provides a lot of entertainment for us all by keeping those TV 'Police Car Crash Bang Wallop Stop! Stop! Caught On CCTV' clip shows in business. No, the really serious crimes are those tiny little offences that are being committed every day. They have a Chinese-water-torture effect, their constant niggling presence making our modern motoring life a misery. Now, it's not really for me to go into devising the most appropriate methods of punishment for people committing the offences listed below, but if anyone's asking, well... I have a few ideas.

"Nice car mate... want to swap?"

People Who Filter From Two Lanes Into One Far Too Early When They Come To Roadworks

You think you're being a decent human being, but you're just doubling the length of the queue. Stay out until the first cone smacks your front bumper and then dive in.

Bass Speakers In The Car Next To You At Traffic Lights Cranked Up To A Teeth-Rattling Volume

Tony Blair would fine the offenders to make more money out of motorists, but no, I have a subtler punishment: impound their cars, replace their ICE systems with an eight-track with a Roger Whittaker tape welded in and the volume knob fixed at ten with barbed wire.

Parents Who Put Their kids In The Rearmost Seats Of Estate Cars, Right By The Back Window

It's not the danger issue: it's what to do when you're stuck behind them in traffic. Most adults are not children's entertainers, and after we've smiled and made a funny face, we're out of ideas. Kids, though, can keep going – for a very long time.

Campers Who Drive From England To Provence With Plastic Garden Chairs On The Roof

Don't do it – you're being really thick. The £8.99 chair will give your car the aerodynamic properties of a quarry face and for the extra money you'll cough up on fuel, you probably could have rented Elton John's villa.

People With Rubbish Cars Who Walk Up To People With Nice Cars And Say, "I'll Swap You."

People Who Live On Really Busy Main Roads

Didn't you think there was a catch when you bought that house with four bedrooms and a big garden for £100? No, it's not the road noise I'm talking about. The real problem is the fact that you cause a ten-mile tailback every time you reverse out of your drive.

And finally, there's one category of car criminals so evil that they deserve a section all of their own: Petrol-Station Tourists. See overleaf for more, if you can take the horror.

Petrol Station Tourists

Without doubt, the most heinous of car criminals are the people who treat a visit to the petrol station as a day out. The point of a petrol station is to dive in, refuel, grab mints, throw money at the man and make a swift exit.

But no. After filling with fuel – usually diesel – these people leave their car blocking the first pump in the row and amble towards the mini-express mart, stopping en route to read all the newspapers in the plastic display stand. Inside, there's no rush to get to the till. First, there's a browse through an atlas of Staffordshire and then a rummage through the bin of BBC comedy cassette tapes. After that, they'll be peckish, but it's no good rushing straight over to the pasties – not when there's tinned stuff to examine first.

That done, it's time to select a pastie, queue up, go outside to check the number of the pump, rejoin the queue, get to the front of the queue, come back out for their Nectar card, rejoin the queue and pay. And then they're done. But no, they're not. It's now time to heat up the pastie they could have had heated up while they were in the queue. This takes a while because an Albanian truck driver will be drying his pants in the microwave. Still, at least that means there's time to get a coffee. There's a choice of instant or fresh-brewed. No prizes for guessing. Naturally, the coffee can't be paid for at the coffee counter, so it's back to the queue. Then, finally paid up, they head for the exit and will be on their way... just as soon as they've extracted maximum pleasure from the Pick'n'Mix counter, and queued up to pay – again.

While they've been gone, another conflict has erupted in the Middle East, oil prices have surged and your toddler's un-strapped himself from the child seat and gone to university. But never mind: our petrol station tourist is now back in the car and ready for the off. And then... nothing happens. While adjusting the rear view mirror, they spot an unruly eyebrow hair, which clearly needs plucking before they can go anywhere. This unleashes a frenzy of pre-flight checks and preparation. No one actually knows what these are. Do they chant for a safe journey? Do they plug in a Hoover and do the carpets? Whatever goes on in there, it takes twenty-five minutes to complete. Eventually they leave and finally you get to the pump. You notice they've put just £10-worth in, which means they'll be back tomorrow.

HOW 2 Have a Mid-Life Crisis

There's nothing wrong with having a mid-life crisis. After all, they usually involve lots of fun, speed and laughter, so why not enjoy a last dose of all that stuff before life becomes a withering spiral of urine-soaked armchairs and daytime telly?

Not only that, but this is possibly the first time you've had the money to do it. The kids hate you and are taking drugs at university, so spend it on yourself by all means. The issue here is not whether to have a mid-life crisis, but how to conduct it, especially with cars, because one of the perpetual puzzlers of life is this: why do people having a mid-life crisis in the bedroom do it with such impeccable discretion, but make such complete cocks of themselves when playing it out through cars?

Just look at the evidence: the mid-life crisis affair is carried out with absolute precision and subterfuge. Every precaution is taken – if you live in Birmingham, you book a hotel in Manchester for your liaison. An extra mobile phone is carried, along with a special credit card. Pockets are checked for incriminating receipts and a small battery-powered vacuum cleaner is always available to remove stray hairs of the wrong shade from clothing. Compare that to the mid-life crisis motorist, sitting at the lights in a bright purple TVR and sporting a pair of ill-advised shades. How can people get it so right on the one hand and so very wrong on the other?

Well, this is a car book and advice concerning complicated and possibly exploitative sexual relationships in later life is, strictly speaking, beyond my remit. And anyway, at least mid-life crisis affairs are conducted in private, so even if you're not very good at it when push comes to shove – as it were – at least push generally comes to shove behind closed doors. The car, though, is something far more public and something I can actually help with. Here, then, is some advice for the mid-life crisis-er who, having organised his affair with the discretion and style of an Italian Count, still needs help with his wheels.

DON'T

"Do as I say, not as I do."

Don't Buy An American Car

See the front cover of this book for what this will do for your style and credibility.

Don't Buy A Lambo And Then Make It Worse

No one blames you for wanting a sports car, but running out and blowing your children's inheritance on a car they once had as a poster on their wall is just not a good idea. They will hate you, other road-users will hate you and your wife or husband will hate you, too. Adorn your ill-advised bauble with a private plate and your lover will also hate you. There is nothing, nothing at all, that can be spelled out with a combination of numbers, letters and carefully-placed bolts to make up for your mistake in buying a car that even Rod Stewart can't carry off.

DIK HD1

Don't Buy A Convertible

Modern convertibles are quiet, draft-proof and sophisticated, but to the successful mid-life motorist they are strictly out of bounds. Be honest: you buy a convertible because you think it will make you look younger, more virile and perhaps a little bit dangerous. You might even be tempted to go for the expensive BOSE stereo upgrade. But sitting there in a traffic jam with the roof down means people can see your bald head and hear your Dire Straits CD. This is not going to achieve what you set out to do. Remember also that while wind-in-the-hair motoring is fine in your twenties, later in life it's just your hair in the wind – vanishing.

Don't Get Busted For Kerb Crawling

It's much more than your expensive alloy wheels that are at risk if you choose to drive too close to the city's kerbs. It's not your rugged good looks and air of confidence and experience that those girls are drawn to.

DO

Audi S8 With V10

This big Audi is a modern car for the modern middle-aged man. Discreet and powerful, with hidden performance capability, it's like a Mach 8 razor with fifteen blades.

It's not all bad news, though. Here is a small selection of cars that are perfectly acceptable as mid-life crisis runabouts: cool, yet still exciting.

Mercedes With Stacked Headlights

Like a moisturizer made from monkey's ears costing tens of thousands of pounds a pot, this really will work – trust us. Slip into this in your fashionable clothes and you will look a million dollars. People will think you're that cool French assassin bloke out of Léon or a Parisian business millionairess looking for a new stable lad.

Ford S-Max With 2.5 Turbo

Okay, so you still need to move the kids around from time to time, but there's no need to despair. This seven-seater is long, low and sleek and actually handles really well. People will appreciate that you still have a caring, nurturing side. You will appreciate the five-cylinder turbocharged engine that goes like heck and the extra space on board for those lunchtime 'meetings' with your PA in that lay-by in Cannock Chase.

Alfa Romeo Spider

The rules of mid-life crisis conduct are different for women. Girls can, for example, be seen in a convertible, and the Spider is the perfect alternative to the footballer's-wife-style Mercedes SLK. Just go and get one then see for yourself what it's like to live in a Jackie Collins novel.

TAKE THE FINAL JOURNEY

And so we come to the final stage in your motoring life. It's time to make the biggest decision of your career as a modern motorist. Let's imagine that fifty years or so from now, you're reading this book. And let's assume that you've carried it with you everywhere and at every crossroads in your life; at every major event, good or bad, you've turned to it for support, wisdom and advice like a kung fu student heeding the words of his master. Fresh-faced and beardless, you consulted it when you bought your first car and were protected by it from the evil intentions of avaricious car dealers. You spent hours locked away with it before emerging calmly into the

sunlight to adorn your Citroën Saxo with chromed tailpipes and spotlights, not heeding the laughter and scorn of your elders because the book said that as a modern motorist you must endure their mockery and become the stronger for it.

Let's assume then that with this book's help, you've played your cards well as a modern motorist. It's time now, though, to hand them in, and the last thing you want to do is to be seen slotted into the back of the wrong ride for the most important car journey of your life – your last one. So why risk blowing it? Think of the indignity. We all put a ton of thought into getting the right wedding car, but, let's be honest, that's something you can always do again. However, the odds are quite well stacked against you ever riding in the back of more than one hearse. Here, then, are some suggestions to help round off your career as a modern motorist with style, if not much actual dignity. And remember, if you're being cremated that's fine, but don't take the book with you and waste all this hard work. Pass it down so others may receive enlightenment.

This is how not to do it. Grey day, grey mourners, grey man in top hat who'd rather walk than sit in British Leyland hearse that will break down.

Just in case you didn't know this car's final destination, it comes with a useful 'No shit Sherlock' illustration...

In truth, only one of the people on this journey is bothered about the speed limit.

George and Mildred's last argument was quite a big one.

Some hearses wake the dead before they're even buried.

If there is life after death, it's your duty to come back and haunt the person who takes you on your last journey in this fashion. There's nothing remotely cool about the hearse having less wheels than the thing that pulls it.

Rule number one: you are the main attraction on this day of days, so don't let the hearse itself steal your thunder. Also, if you go for the steam-driven option, you'll start to smell by the time you get there.

If you have a lot of friends, make provision in your will for a bigger hearse. Only Monty Don would be happy with this arrangement.

The
Knowledge

The Top 5 Amazing Car Stunts

Car adverts, as we know, are some of the best in the world. Indeed, the sixties ads for the Beetle in America are generally considered to have invented the whole art form of modern, intelligent advertising. Sadly, by the time the car gets into the hands of the dealer, his efforts to introduce a car to the public are altogether rather more, er, pikey. His launch plan will invariably include a photograph in the local paper of him handing a giant key to the assistant director of the local Chamber of Commerce and a dealer launch extravaganza evening with a Hawaiian theme and entertainment from his son's band, who aren't from Hawaii. The climax will be the presentation of a free GL model with the dealer's name sign-written down the side to Rusty Lee.

But in between the glossy TV commercial and the crappy dealer's efforts, there's a sub-culture of the Amazing Car Stunt. Within the car company these are the work of people who are, well, they're like the Tom Hanks' character in Big and we wish they would run the whole operation. Here's five of the best ...

1 CORTINA

This was one of the very first of these clever stunts, excluding all the ones before it. The Cortina was Ford's glamorous car for the common man and as such, went on to become an enormous success. Its glamorous appeal lay in its name. At the time, the notion of foreign travel was just beginning to implant itself in the minds of the masses. Glossy magazines were full of skinny models in far-flung places and James Bond films were as much about glamorous locations as Bond getting his willy fried by a laser.

Ford wanted to give their new car a glamorous, jet set lifestyle image, which is why they named it after somewhere abroad when every other model had dreary, somewhat drab names such as Wolseley, Humber and Snipe. So, for the launch stunt in December 1964, Ford took the Cortina to the Cortina Bobsleigh Run and had rally driver Henry Taylor drive it down.

2 AUDI

With the Quattro Audi had brought the concept of four-wheel drive road cars to the masses and consequently they were keen to capitalise on its success with every succeeding model. The rather humdrum Audi 100 really didn't compete in any way with the fiery Quattro, except that it had doors and wheels, but that didn't deter Audi. So, by way of giving this family motor a bit of extra sparkle at the 1980 launch, it was driven up a ski ramp. What they failed to do, however, was to send it back down again with rockets on the back, which would have been so much more clever.

3   CMG

When General Motors launched the GMC Jimmy SLT – a compact SUV – in 1993, bungee jumping had become a worldwide craze. What better way to get the message across to rednecks that this car can accommodate five hogs, three murder victims and a barrel of moonshine than to bungee jump it off a big bridge? They did, it bounced and they pulled it back up again. Note: It is difficult, in a still photograph, to show the drama of this event. For maximum effect, hold the book open at this page and drop it onto a mattress. Watch as the first goes downward and then bounces back up again. Well, it was a bit like that.

4   ANDRE CITROËN

In the car world Andre Citroën was the master of innovative stunts. A shy man, he lit up the Eiffel Tower with his own name and when people complained about the commercialism, Citroën persuaded Charles Lindbergh to claim the lights had helped guide him during his flight. He sponsored road signs throughout France in the name of Citroën and was the first to introduce toy versions of his own cars to get children hooked as early as possible. So when, in 1934, he decided the best way to launch the amazingly forward-looking new Citroën Traction Avant was to have it driven off a cliff, no one was that surprised. The car survived the drop and, incredibly, was driven away.

5 LAND ROVER UP DAM

It's difficult to find places in Birmingham, where Land Rover is made, to show off the car's off-road prowess so the company took their brand-new short wheelbase 90 to Wales, near England, for a spectacular launch stunt.

Richard Hammond's Top Models

Fastest ▶ BUGATTI VEYRON

In the same way that the sun is hotter than other radiators, the Bugatti Veyron is faster than other road cars. And not only is it more beautiful and powerful than anything else, it's also a minefield of near-pornographic automotive trivia.

The figures are huge: it's got 1,001 bhp, the top speed is quoted at 253 mph, and if you want to buy one it will set you back £700,000. But then there are other figures that are all the more impressive for being tiny: the sequential gearbox can shift gear in 0.2 seconds, accelerating to 60 mph takes three seconds, and even getting to 180 mph takes just fourteen.

Creating an engine that can produce 1,001 bhp is tricky. To make that kind of power it must burn through nearly one and half gallons of fuel every sixty seconds. The W16 engine – two V8s stuck together – can do this, and at full speed the tank will be empty in just fifteen minutes. But the Veyron's engine can't punch its way through the air – above 220 mph, each tiny notch of extra speed gets incredibly hard to eke out on the strength of cubic capacity alone, so it has turbos: four of them. That in turns means lots of cooling issues, so there are also ten radiators. Of course, it's impossible to send 1,001 bhp through an ordinary gearbox – that would be like a champion weight lifter passing the dumbbells to a 6-year-old while he did up his laces – so they designed a special, seven-speed gearbox with two clutches. And that much power going to just two wheels would mean the Veyron simply sitting there and digging a hole to Australia, so they made it a permanent four-wheel drive.

Now, if you want to go for a top-speed run, Bugatti don't make it easy. First, you have to phone them and tell them, and then you have to turn a special key that locks all the wings and diffusers into a special setting. Then you need a straight road – something over sixty miles long with no bends. So that'll be Australia then. But beware: once you get up to 253 mph, no one knows how long the tyres will last – after 15 minutes they could disintegrate, so you'd better hope you run out of petrol first.

Most Advanced → MERCEDES S CLASS

The S Class is most famous for being the favourite runabout of tyrants and dictators the world over. But dictators aren't that imaginative – look at Kim Jung Il's wardrobe – and they all choose their car on a Keeping Up With the Pol Pots basis, which means they all have S Classes. And they're so busy specifying anti-grenade body panels they probably don't realise they've already got the most technically advanced car on the planet. The newest S Class is quite simply mind-blowing. It has cruise control, obviously, but there's much more to it than that. This car sees through fog, reads the distance to the car ahead, and automatically applies the brake without you doing a thing. The radar it shoots out to perform this task is on the same frequency as military missile hardware and it took Mercedes years to get clearance. It's at night when the boffins really earn their money, though, because the world's first infrared headlamps will feed a perfect image of the road ahead onto a screen in your car, making all past attempts at lighting the way completely redundant.

If all this safety stuff isn't enough to keep you from having a crash then when the fateful moment comes, you've got the best chance of surviving in the S Class. Just before it all goes horribly wrong, the sensors in the car will read the situation and literally take over, whipping your seat into the best position, tightening seat belts and priming air bags, all in the blink of an eye. Then, when you leave hospital, you can treat yourself to a massage from the S Class's built-in seat massager… and we're not talking about a stick-on-a-motor poking through the seat back. Oh, no! You can choose from settings such as 'Fast and Vigorous' or 'Slow and Gentle' – they really are running out of things to invent.

Irv Gordon has driven just under 2.5 million miles in his 1966 Volvo P1800.
Even if the Lunar Rover mentioned in the next section were eligible to enter (it isn't, because it didn't travel to space under its own power) it would still lose: Irv's Volvo has done the equivalent of four and a half return trips to the moon. It still has its original engine and transmission and has gone through 6,667 oil changes and 400 spark plugs.

To equal Irv's record would mean driving at a steady 50 mph for 44,000 hours. He was the first man in the USA to pass the two million mile mark and still drives his Volvo every day, averaging one thousand miles a week. You've got to spare a thought for the poor guy: still the damn thing won't die.

IRV'S TIPS FOR INTERSTELLAR CAR MILEAGE

Start with a car you really like: "If you don't like your car, you'll never go the distance." So why did you start with a Volvo, Irv?

Spend a few minutes a week checking under the bonnet: "Even the most mechanically challenged car owners can look for low fluid levels or deterioration of belts and hoses." Ever looked under the bonnet of a modern car?

Wax at least twice a year: "It provides protection against oxidation and rust." So, you've got great legs, how will that help my car last longer?

Develop a good relationship with your dealer and mechanic: "Both are your partners in the long run." Er, right, is this a physical thing?

Use petrol from a high-volume station: 'Without heavy traffic, petrol remains in storage units for long periods of time.' Just imagine the Nectar points…

When your car makes a funny noise, listen to it: "The longer you wait, the greater potential for damage." What if it's supposed to sound like that?

Fastest Selling → MUSTANG

That the Mustang became the fastest-ever seller on the day it was launched may have been down to its appeal as a cheap and stylish car, or just another example of the power of those advertising types with clever glasses. At precisely 9:30pm on the evening of 16 April 1964, whichever of the three American TV networks viewers were tuned in to, they all saw the same thing. Ford had 'road blocked' all three channels to advertise the launch of the brand-new Mustang

The following morning, sales went berserk. Dealerships all over the country had queues stretching round the block. Fat, sweaty car dealers must barely have had time to pop a donut in their mouths in between being oily to punters desperate to hand over their $2,500. The Mustang was first thought up in 1961 by Lee Iacocca, vice president and general manager of the Ford Division. He wanted to make a cheap car that would accommodate four people in bucket seats, with sporty performance, a floor-mounted shifter and a wheelbase of no more than 180 inches. In an era when great, finned land yachts were still wobbling around the country, this sharp little sports car must have come as a refreshing change. And the pressure didn't let up, either – by the end of its first year, 418,812 Mustangs had been sold.

New Ford Mustang $2368 f.o.b. Detroit

FORD

Biggest ▶ THE RAINBOW SHEIKH'S PICK-UP

In the desert, objects have no scale – so when you first see the pick-up, you don't realise it's still another two miles away. It's only when you get close up that the penny drops and then your head explodes.

The pick-up lives in the desert of the United Arab Emirates and belongs to the Rainbow Sheikh, a car nut who also has a fleet of Mercedes – each one a different colour of the rainbow. It's based on a 1940s Dodge Power Wagon and was built as a tribute to that original vehicle because it was the one machine capable of exploring for oil in the untamed Empty Quarter desert. But you're probably not interested in that. What you really want to know is that the Sheikh's machine is sixty-four times bigger than the original and tall enough to fit a Range Rover underneath. It is a working vehicle and it does move, thanks to an engine from an earth-mover, but its primary purpose is as a desert caravan. Behind the radiator grille is one bedroom, and behind the windscreen is another. Work your way down through the truck and you'll find a kitchen, a bathroom, two more bedrooms and, at the back, the living room, where the tailgate drops down to make a patio.

Most Beautiful ➔ LAMBORGHINI MIURA

Plenty of cars can be called beautiful, and with its sleek lines, elegant proportions and bold curves, the Miura is certainly among them. But that's not what makes it the most beautiful ever. The Miura wins that accolade because it brought something else to the party. This was not some silicone-enhanced improvement on previous beauties. When it arrived in the sixties, it was a groundbreaker. Imagine standing outside your terraced house on your black-and-white high street in 1966, your tank-top chafing at the neck, as a bright citrus-yellow Miura rumbled past the grey ranks of Morris Minors and Ford Anglias. It must have looked as if it had come from outer space.

Where it actually originated from was the imaginations of a group of 20-something Lamborghini designers, who worked in their spare time in the evenings and at weekends to create something they believed in. This car was born of passion. Experts can analyse the gear ratios and torque curves, praise the balance of its shape, even postulate that the 'eyelashes' around the headlights soften the beauty of it, making it more approachable – human, even. The simple truth is, just stand back and take a look at it. Forty years on, it still hasn't been surpassed.

Scariest → SCHAUFELRADBAGGER

The name Schaufelradbagger literally means 'scoop wheel excavator', but that's a poor name for this leviathan and does nothing to convey the sheer terror it instils in everything this side of a Klingon invasion fleet. Weighing in at 45,000 tonnes, it is 100 metres high and 217 metres long; just the shadow of it would be enough to empty a city. Be unlucky enough to get close up to it, and you would be well advised to keep clear of the business end, where the spinning 22-metre wheel with its twenty scoops can tear enough coal from the poor, quivering planet in a day to fill 100,000 dump trucks. Not to be taken lightly, this sort of destructive force needs five people to operate it and moves on twelve crawler units. Mind you, if it does decide to give chase you can probably outrun it. Top speed is just one mile in three hours.

Richard Hammond's
Worst
Models

Ugliest ➤ THE AURORA

Since Benz built his very first car in 1885, countless thousands of car types have been created, so the winner of the coveted 'Ugliest Car Ever' title has to be a minger of ultra proportions – and that would be the Aurora. Built in 1957 by a Catholic priest who really should have stuck to dispensing Hail Marys, on the way down the Aurora didn't just hit every branch of the Ugly Tree, it also went on to hit the ugly soil, the surrounding ugly boulders, and then ran into Ugly Town to hit everything there.

It's hard to know where to start with this car. It really is hard because most people could never tell whether it was going forward or reversing. Down the sides, the dominant motif seems to be giant slugs, and the front grille looks vaguely like Wallace and Gromit smiling for the camera. But the *pièce de résistance* is the collapsed pudding that is the fibreglass roof. The car took Father Alfred Juliano three years and $30,000 to make; it seems he was obsessed with saving lives as well as souls. Safety features abounded, including foam-filled bumpers, rollover bars and a seat that swivelled 180° degrees in a crash. Why? Anyway, no one bought it, and today it's so ugly it's almost beautiful.

Worst to Drive → LEYAT

With no shortage of un-driveable heaps being produced through the decades, this is another hotly contested category. And there are a few surprises too. The Ford Model T might have sold 15 million, but try driving one today and you're likely to park it up a tree. All the pedals are in the wrong place, so it's like driving with your legs crossed. But at the time it was built, there was no established layout, so we can't blame ol' Henry on this occasion. The Lancia Stratos might be a motor racing legend, but it was also a driving nightmare. With a wide track and super-short wheelbase, it was almost impossible to drive in a straight line - great for rallying, hopeless on the high street.

And it gets much worse than that. There have been gyro-cars that didn't gyro, cars with tillers instead of steering wheels, the Rolls Royce limited to the top speed of its day of 12mph, cars you drive while perched on the roof and cars with brakes only operating on one wheel. But I have to pick a winner here and for sheer undriveability, I am going to go for the Leyat. This French horror used a radial engine to power a wooden propeller at the front. This meant not only that it was awful to drive as the poor pilot had to peer through the spinning prop, it was also pretty awful for pedestrians in an accident. And there were a lot of accidents with these things. It was inherently unstable and so basically turned into a giant, out-of-control food blender rampaging along the street. A particularly unpleasant experience was hitting a goose, as it would pass through the propeller before showering down on the unfortunate driver.

Most Embarassing ➤ THE ELECTRIC SHOPPER

This is a tough one, with several worthy candidates vying for the gold.
The AMC Pacer, for example, hardly marks you out as Donald Trump, and then there's
the Peel car, the Isle of Man's finest automotive offering. But the main thing here is how
much of an idiot the particular car makes you look, and the Pacer became cool with
Wayne's World, so out it goes. Besides looking wretched, the Peel has no reverse gear so
you have to get out and physically turn it round, which is pretty embarrassing. The trouble
is no one minds in a gnomey place like the Isle of Man. So, that leaves only one winner:
The Electric Shopper. It was built in California between 1952 and 1962, and can you
imagine how you would have looked cruising down to Venice beach in this thing
surrounded by sleek, big-finned Cadillacs? At a time when no one had even invented the
fuel crisis, what was the point? With a massive 1.5 bhp on offer, its top speed was a
heady 18 mph, which gave everyone plenty of time to laugh as
you pottered by. Mercifully, it only had a range of thirty miles,
so the misery
would be over in
just over ninety
minutes.

Most Scandalous ➔ FORD PINTO

The harmless-looking Ford Pinto was one of the best-selling cars of the seventies. A humdrum sort of a thing, it was available as a two-door coupé or hatchback, with simple suspension and a 1.6-litre engine. However, it turned out to be the fiery demon that could have brought Ford crashing to its knees. You see, when involved in an accident, the Pinto had a nasty habit of bursting into flames and killing everyone inside. The problem was a faulty fuel tank. As the Pinto didn't have a proper rear bumper, it was easy for the tank to be pushed forwards in a rear-end shunt, where protruding bolts could spike holes in it with inevitable and terrible consequences. This was bad. What made it worse was a tendency for the doors to jam shut due to poor reinforcing, which was very, very bad. Worse still was the fact that Ford knew about the problem and chose to do nothing about it.

The company made one of the most hard-nosed, cost-benefit analyses in automotive history. Ford estimated that the faulty Pinto would cause 180 deaths per year. Company engineers calculated that it would cost $11 per car to fix the problem – a total cost of $137 million. However, Ford put a value of $200,000 on each of the lives lost, based on loss of wages, medical and legal costs, which meant a total cost of $36 million. In other words, Ford decided it was cheaper to pay the compensation than it was to fix the faulty petrol tank at $11 a car. In 1977, new fuel-tank safety regulations were introduced and Ford immediately fixed the Pinto. But word had got out about the company's secret, calculated gamble and after that it was, unsurprisingly, a less than popular car. The Pinto eventually breathed its last in 1980.

Oh! almost forgot to mention that the fuel tank is only protected from any impact you may happen to encounter by a flimsy bit of chrome more commonly known on other vehicles as a bumper

PLATFORM CONSTRUCTION

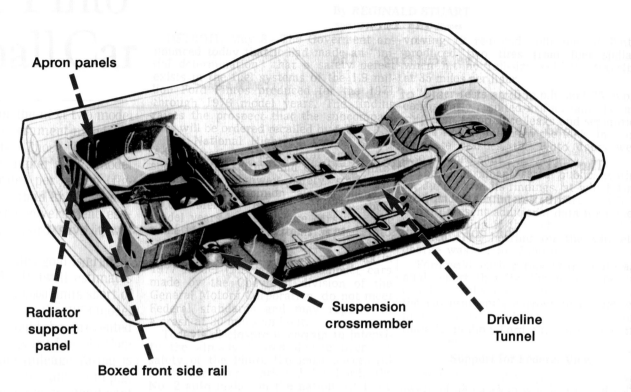

Apron panels

Radiator
support
panel

Boxed front side rail

Suspension
crossmember

Driveline
Tunnel

Worst Value for Money ➤ LUNAR ROVER

If we're judging a car on pure cost, then the Lunar Rover makes the Veyron look like a Korean import. Only four were ever built, at a cost of $38 million, bringing each car in at $12.5 million. The Rovers went on three moon landings – Apollos 15, 16 and 17. Between them they covered just fifty miles, meaning each mile cost $760,000. For that money you'd expect some pretty thrilling motoring, but the top speed of the Rover was only 8 mph, thanks to each wheel having only a quarter of a horsepower fed to it. There were no optional extras, and the only thing you could play with was the adjustable footrest. The only other groovy bits were the wheels: no naff rubber for these boys. Instead the tyres were made of zinc-coated woven steel with titanium chevrons on the outside to provide tread. I don't know if that was the best way to go about it, but it sounds great. The point of the Lunar Rover was to help astronauts get about more easily because the bulkiness of their space suits meant it took them ages to walk anywhere to collect rocks and stuff. But to be honest, was it worth it? It's not as if they found some aliens and had a space gun battle or anything.

You are here

Most Vulgar → 100ft LIMO

Welcome to hen-night heaven. At almost 35 metres, this is the longest limo in the world and the longest car ever built. It has twenty-six wheels and two engines, one in the front and one in the back. Surprisingly, it wasn't handcrafted in a traditional workshop in the Malvern hills, but was built by Jay Ohrenberg of Burbank, California. A huge, gaudy symbol of American excess, some limos have hot tubs in the back and this one has a swimming pool with diving board. Other handy, on-board extras include a king-sized waterbed and a heli-pad. Party-organizers shouldn't be put off by the length: it can be driven as a rigid vehicle or made to bend in the middle – so the streets of Newcastle should be no problem.

Strange Laws and Customs

I don't want to come over all Alf Garnett here, but it's a sad truth that Britain is now overrun with daft laws. One day it could be the EU telling us we can't eat prawn cocktail crisps unless we're wearing black tie on a full moon, the next it'll be Tony Blair banning playground conkers unless the children are wearing riot gear. But the thing is, we're not alone. Plenty of other countries out there are also laying down ridiculous laws as banana skins on the pavement of life...

In China's Beijing City, it's an offence for a driver to stop at a pedestrian crossing. Halting to let a pedestrian cross is punishable with a fine – I don't know why either. Mind you, it's better than the old days. In 1920s Beijing, the penalty for speeding was beheading…

…and sticking with the Liberal Democrats, drunk drivers in El Salvador face death by firing squad.

But if a man is convicted of drink-driving in Malaysia, his wife is also thrown in the slammer for co-responsibility.

In Germany it's an offence to make derogatory signs at other drivers. You can invade neighbouring countries, though.

In Vancouver, a law still exists requiring all motorists to carry anchors in their cars, to be used as emergency brakes.

Until recently it was necessary for women in Lithuania to undergo a gynaecological examination before qualifying for a driving licence.

Hula-Hoops were banned in Japan in the 1950s because they caused so many accidents among motorists craning their necks to watch people using them.

The size of a speeding fine in Finland is proportional to your income. Spare a thought then for Jussi Salonaja, the 27-year-old heir to a sausage empire, who was caught doing 80 kph in a 40-kph zone and fined £120,000, the highest speeding fine ever recorded in the country. The previous record was a mere £50,000, paid by a dot-com entrepreneur.

In Russel, Kansas, it's against the law to have a musical car horn.

In Evanston, Illinois, it's illegal to change any of your clothes inside a car – unless there's a fire.

In Somalia, it's an offence to drive with a lump of old chewing gum attached to your nose.

In Denmark, it's illegal to start your car before checking whether anyone's underneath it.

In Saudi Arabia, a 16-year-old male can drive a car if accompanied by any qualified male. Having his mother in the car – if she is the only person – is not allowed. However, if it's his sister, that's okay. But if it's a female who's not a blood relative, that's a complete no-no.

Hitchhiking in Colorado can fetch a two-year jail sentence.

The Czech Republic forbids any person under 1.5 metres tall from travelling in the front seat.

In **Cottonwood, Arizona,** it's illegal to make love in a car… with flat tyres. The fine is $25 if the car is parked, and $100 if you're still on the move.

Sex matters are much more relaxed in Germany. When a man recently appeared in a Cologne court for hitting a road sign at 60 mph while having sex with a hitchhiker, he was merely fined for leaving the scene of an accident.

Singapore's an odd one. Staying with the matter of vehicular rumpy-pumpy, the law states that oral sex is illegal in a car, "unless used only as a form of foreplay". Mind you, towing another car is strictly against the law and even owning a car with a towbar can bring on a fine. Caravanning enthusiasts, take note.

It's illegal for a car to backfire in Rutland, Vermont.

In Coeur d'Alene, Idaho, the police are much more discreet about car-based copulation. If a police officer suspects some suspension-spring bashing is underway in a vehicle, he must pull up from behind, sound his car hooter three times and then wait two minutes before investigating.

In Sweden, a loophole in the law allows cars to be registered in childrens' names. This normally works okay – until you get cases such as the recent one where a 10-year-old in Stockholm was billed £27,000 for traffic fines.

Until recently, the driving test in Egypt consisted of driving 100 metres forward between two cones and then reversing back through them. Wouldn't you just like to meet the person who failed it?

In laugh-a-minute Switzerland, you can be prosecuted for washing your car on a Sunday, for not turning off your engine at traffic lights and for leaving your keys in your car – but only if the car door is open. Hiding Nazi gold in bank vaults is okay, though.

In Tremonton, Utah, no woman is allowed to have sex with a man while riding in an ambulance.

Macedonia is very tough on drink-driving. Not only is it illegal for the driver to be over the limit, but even the front seat passenger must not have drunk any alcohol. This means Macedonians on nights out have to nominate both a designated driver and a designated front-seat passenger.

All sheep in the cab of your truck must be accompanied by a chaperone in Missouri.

It's customary for drink-drivers in Turkey to be driven 20 miles out of town by the police and made to walk home while being jeered at by a police escort.

In Japan, a senior official of the National Police Agency recently declared that if the 'Don't Walk' sign starts flashing when a pedestrian is forty-nine per cent of the way across a pedestrian crossing they should turn back – what a scream he must be at dinner parties.

In happy-go-lucky Frederick, Maryland, driver Ester Maria Peña was arrested and handcuffed for doing 38 mph on a 55-mph limit road. Actually, that's pretty fair…

In Tennessee it is illegal to drive while sleeping…

…while in Clinton, Oklahoma, it's an offence to "molest an automobile".

And finally...

in San Francisco, it's illegal to wipe the exterior of your car with used underwear. Unused underwear, however, is fine.

Road Signs

The conditions are terrible, and you're crawling up the motorway at six miles per hour, barely able to make out the fog lights of the truck two metres ahead of you. After a while, you notice a goulish orange glow off to the right. As you inch up the motorway towards it, the light splits into three weird shapes. Straining your eyes to see through the gloom, you eventually make out the word "FOG". Well, thanks. That's as much use as the lookout who, after the ship smashes into the rocks and dashes itself to pieces, shouts "Land-ho".

Road signs can, of course, be terribly useful. Knowing there's a Little Chef ahead, or even somewhere to eat, can be invaluable. But being told it's a good idea to take a break if your eyes keep closing or warned that a big rock might at any time land on your roof is not. What are you supposed to do about the rocks anyway? Wear a helmet.

The stupid road sign is not a phenomenon limited to the UK. Over the page is a bumper crop of international information idiocy. By all means spend a few hours of your life devising funny captions for them all. Only please, please don't send them to me.

You could be forgiven for slamming your foot on the brakes when seeing this sign, but no, there isn't a speed camera ahead. Instead, the United States authorities are kindly pointing out that there's a nice view somewhere just up the road that you might like to stop and photograph. Well I'll be the judge of that, thanks. I might prefer photographing fish actually. Or nudes.

And this is not a forecast warning you of a windy day ahead, but a warning to motorists in San Diego about Mexicans dashing across the road to freedom. In bandanas.

Noble Failures

These days cars may work pretty well and can even survive 1,000 mph crashes while making all the flowers smile as they drive by, but the thing is, they are in the main white goods. They're all much of a muchness, and the big car companies only care about market share and hair gel. There was a time, though, when real risks were taken, in an attempt to impress potential customers.

Dodge La Femme

America, 1955 – and if ever Germaine Greer was needed, it was now. Over at Chrysler HQ in Detroit, a boardroom full of men decided that there was a need for a car that appealed to women, and so the Dodge La Femme was born. Completely ignoring the fact that women had spent the previous decade or two emancipating themselves, the La Femme sailed into the showroom boasting pink paintwork in a choice of shades: 'Heather Rose', 'Misty Orchid' or 'Regal Orchid'. The trim was pale pink, the upholstery featured pink rosebuds, the carpets were pink... you get the picture. Just in case anyone remained in any doubt that the La Femme was aimed at women, standard equipment included a purse containing a compact and lipstick, and a pink rain mac, bonnet and umbrella. Launched in 1955 to great fanfare, the La Femme unsurprisingly sank without trace two years later, with just 2,500 having been sold – or maybe that should read, "with, *amazingly*, 2,500 having been sold".

The Shamrock

This is one of those cars that fell down the back of the sofa of history – and it's really not hard to see why. The Shamrock was the brainchild of an Irish-American chap called Wilbur Curtis. His plan was to build, in Southern Ireland, a car that resembled an American car, but reeked of the Old Country. Curtis was convinced that when they saw its green-flock dashboard and shamrock badge, misty-eyed expats in Boston and New York would queue round the block to shell out. And maybe they would have done. But then he built the car that he built… The first problem was the power: a 1.5-litre, 53-bhp engine in a car seventeen feet long was never going to impress Bostonians used to huge V8s. Unfortunately, the chassis was also based on a tiny Austin A55, which meant the car was twice the length of its wheelbase and cornered like a drunken oil rig. And if you did corner quickly, the fibreglass body would flex so much that the door flew open.

Round the back, things weren't much better: the car sat so low that it wouldn't jack up high enough to let you change the rear tyres if you had a puncture. But that was okay, because the boot didn't open enough to allow you to put a spare tyre in anyway. Curtis gamely set up production in 1959, using green card-table baize to cover the dash and employing the local tailor to cut patterns for the body moulds. Inevitably, he closed down a year later.

The Dunkley

We could criticise the Dunkley for the fact that it's made from knitting needles and old wicker baskets, but the bigger problem was that it wasn't exactly popular with courting couples. It could be driven from either end, though – which, again, was a pretty pointless feature.

The Wolseley Silent Six

It's not so much the car that's the problem here as the advertising campaign that went with it. The Silent Six was a relatively normal car launched in 1926 by engineers who gave it this particular name because they were so proud of the relative silence of its six-cylinder engine. To this end, the bonnet mascot featured six men in hooded robes, looking suspiciously like Ku Klux Klan members. Wolseley innocently believed people would see them as monks in a silent order, but as a business *faux pas* it was up there with Gerald Ratner's "crap" cock-up. And to make matters worse, the publicity stills featured Wolseley workers outside the factory gates, also dressed in white robes and hoods. Soon after, with sales not even taking off in Alabama, the car was re-branded and went on to sell rather well.

Edsel

The Edsel started out as one of Ford's biggest and most ambitious ventures, but ended up being dubiously renowned as the biggest flop in motoring history. As you would expect, considerable thought went into the name of the thing – at least in the beginning. One young spark even invited a poet to name the car, but she turned out to be something of a space cadet, and made suggestions such as 'Mongoose Civique', 'Intelligent Whale' and 'Utopian Turtletop'. By the time she had been thanked for her efforts and removed from the building, the Ford executives had run out of steam, and reluctantly settled for 'Edsel'.

The car was launched in 1958 to great fanfare, and offered more options than any other car around – including a futuristic push-button gear change system in the middle of the steering wheel. However, the cars were badly built and broke down. A lot. Then a problem unforeseen by Ford arose: Americans shunned the Edsel because the shape of the radiator grille reminded them of a lady's intimate area. Ford fought to rescue the situation and an Edsel TV variety spectacular hosted by Bing Crosby and Frank Sinatra was watched by 53 million viewers, but shifted no Edsels. The next desperate move was to make dealers give away ponies, which just caused the price of ponies to skyrocket once horse traders latched onto the situation. Eventually, after just three years, the car was killed off, having cost Ford an estimated $250 million. That's $1.7 billion at today's prices.

Chrysler Turbine

In the fifties and sixties, Americans were obsessed with space travel, speed records, jet engines... basically anything that would make them go faster than the goddam Commies – hence the incredible Chrysler Turbine. This car was powered by adapted aircraft turbine engines, and on the move it sounded and felt like it: the heat from the turbine pipe alone was hot enough to ignite paper. The engine had hardly any moving parts, delivered instant torque and revved to an unbelievable 60,000 rpm. Turbines would take almost any fuel, too, and when the President of Mexico borrowed one he proved the point by running it on Tequila. Chrysler wanted to make the car, but it would have cost hundreds of millions of dollars to re-tool factories and gear up dealerships to service them. In the end, fifty were made, and they were loaned out secretly to American families for a while, but then all but two were destroyed.

Richard eagerly awaits the horse's verdict on the Edsel.

Purves Dynasphere

Dr Purves really should have known better. I mean, by the time the daring engineer built this contraption in the thirties, the car as we know it had been around for a while and he must have seen that everyone was quite happy to actually sit on a normal seat in the car rather than in one of the wheels. Maybe as a child he was abandoned by his parents and raised by guinea pigs, who knows? The Dynasphere never caught on, but fair's fair, it worked. John Purves took his inspiration from designs originally drawn

up by Leonardo Da Vinci, and when he demonstrated it at Brooklands race circuit and on south-coast beaches, he got it up to a giddy 25 mph. That was plenty though, because the Dynasphere wasn't very good at steering and braking, which is a bit of a problem when you're trying to persuade the public that your form of transport has the edge over a normal car. Stopping was particularly hairy because if the passenger braked too harshly, he would simply be flipped round and round the inside of the wheel like a hamster on crack.

Panther Solo

This had all the ingredients of a great British supercar. Its wild looks were the work of the stylists responsible for the Aston Martin Virage, the engine was from a Sierra Cosworth, it had four-wheel drive, and on its launch in 1989 the Solo had the most advanced body materials – Kevlar, carbon – yet seen on a production car.

Unfortunately, the fit and finish were poor and even stockbrokers wouldn't pay the £40,000 asking price. Just twelve were sold before yet another British sports car bit the dust.

The Wolseley Gyro Car

In 1912, no one, but no one, among the general public was asking for a car that could keep itself upright on just two wheels. Nevertheless, boffins set about the task and the Wolseley Gyro was the result. Weighing an astonishing three tons, it required a massive dynamo to power the equally humongous gyroscope that kept the car upright. It worked rather well, but the thing is, nobody gave a toss.

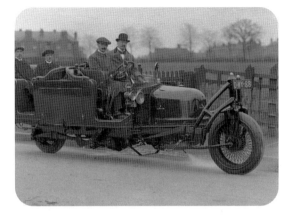

The Dymaxion Car

A bit of a sad failure, this one – mad as it sounds, the Dymaxion wasn't the product of crackpot engineering, but instead built to sound principles that were decades ahead of their time. The teardrop shape was the key innovation, giving this thirties car an aerodynamic smoothness that made every other machine on the road resemble two tortoises having a fight. So smooth was the body enclosing even the wheels that the Dymaxion could do 120 mph on a 90-bhp engine – normal cars would need 300 bhp to achieve that. Okay, it only had three wheels and you had to use a periscope to see out the back, but Cindy Crawford's got a mole, you know.

All was going well for the car until a prominent British aero enthusiast drove it and was killed when it crashed. After that the project was canned, but in aerodynamics terms the Dymaxion showed the way forward.

Pub Quiz Trivia

Let's suppose, as often happens, that one night you're driving over the moors and your car breaks down outside The Howling Wolf during a full moon. The landlord says you can take your chances out on the moors, or stay at the inn as long as you take part in that night's motoring pub quiz. Well, you'd want to be prepared, wouldn't you? Or, let's just say – as can happen – that you're an astronaut on the space station and you have one of those historic East meets West moments when your spaceship docks with the Russian vessel. Once you've exchanged flags and eaten some toothpaste, the Russians say, "Who's for a car quizski then?" Again, it's scout motto time. Admittedly it's hard to become an astronaut, but a much more likely scenario is that you meet Halle Berry and Jennifer Lopez in your local branch of Nando's and they invite you back for a threesome, on one condition... first, you must play strip car-quiz-trivia poker. Well, you might not want to miss out on that – especially if you're a chap – so, over the next few pages you'll find some golden nuggets of car trivia. And we're not talking rubbish here: these are the best prime fillets, with just a little bit of fat left in for flavour.

1 Car companies love endorsements from celebrities, but the all-time most bizarre must surely be the letter from Bonnie and Clyde to Henry Ford. At the height of their bank-emptying careers, the two mid-West outlaws wrote to Ford praising his V8 model for being such a great getaway car. Shortly afterwards, Bonnie and Clyde were filled full of lead by Plod, but not being one to miss a trick, Ford used their letter in an ad campaign.

Tulsa Okla
10th April

Mr. Henry Ford
Detroit Mich.

Dear Sir:—
While I still have got breath in my lungs I will tell you what a dandy car you make. I have drove Fords exclusively when I could get away with one. For sustained speed and freedom from trouble the Ford has got ever other car skinned and even if my business haven't been strickly legal it don't hurt eny thing to tell you what a fine car you got in the V8—

Yours truly
Clyde Champion Barrow

2 Michael Caine hadn't taken his driving test when he made *The Italian Job*.

3 In September 1914, World War I was under way and Paris was under threat from the advancing German army. French Commander General Gallieni needed to move his troops quickly from Paris to Meaux in order to see off Jerry, but he had no transport available. So he ordered 1,300 taxis, into which he crammed 4,000 troops, promised the drivers the fare plus a third, drove into battle and saved the day.

4 The invention of the car revolutionised courting among young couples. Henry Ford allegedly designed the Model T's back seat so that it would be too uncomfortable for boy-girl mischief, but he was onto a loser: in post-war America more than 40 per cent of marriage proposals took place in drive-in cinemas.

6 This nasty Soviet Bloc car, the ZAZ 966, came with possibly the most unusual car accessory of all time – a trapdoor in the floor that enabled drivers to fish on frozen lakes without leaving their cars.

7 The VW Beetle, the world's biggest-selling car of all time, would never have existed if it hadn't been for a British Army soldier from Yorkshire. In 1945, with Germany in ruins, Major Ivan Hirst was given the job of looking after the shattered and bombed Volkswagen factory in Wolfsburg. No one expected him to actually do anything with it, but he rounded up the locals, got the machinery going and started turning out cars held together partly by fish glue. Henry Ford was offered the factory, but when he saw the Beetle, he declared it a dead loss. So far, it's sold over 20 million and counting.

8 Legend has it that the reason we Brits drive on the left is down to Napoleon. The vertically challenged warmonger saw how the peasants drove around in chaotic fashion on the French roads and decreed the road should be split down the middle and that everyone should travel on the right. The British authorities then heard about this, and grudgingly admitted it was a good idea – but because they hated the French, they decided we should travel on the left.

9 The Jaguar XJ40 is a beautiful model, renowned among other things for its sloping back. But that rear end wasn't actually part of the plan. The finished clay model of the car was transported from one Jaguar base to another and the back end sagged en route. Unfortunately all the pressing moulds for the actual car were made from the measurements of the clay model, so that's the car we got.

10 Throughout the thirties, forties and fifties, the first air-conditioning units were very popular after-sales options. Basically a smaller version of the 'swamp coolers' that many Californians had on the roofs of their houses, the Thermador Car-Cooler was a large, metal canister with another, smaller canister inside that contained balsa shavings held in place with mesh. Before setting off, the unit was filled with water and when passengers felt the need for its cooling effect, they would pull a string hanging down inside the car, which would rotate the inner canister of balsa shavings through the water. Wind blowing in through the open end of the unit was cooled by water soaked balsa before being directed into the cabin. Apparently it worked surprisingly well.

11 As enthusiasts might tell you, four-wheel drive for road cars was not pioneered by Audi, but in fact first appeared on the West Bromwich-built Jensen FF, which was based on the same company's two-wheel drive Interceptor. Power from the huge 6276cc V8 engine was fed to all four wheels using the 'Ferguson Formula' four-wheel drive system, making the Interceptor FF a formidable sports car years ahead of its time. Sadly, it did not sell well, and only 320 were ever built.

12 Legendary cigar-sucker Winston Churchill could be credited with inventing the tank, or at least the concept. Churchill came up with the idea that vehicles with caterpillar tracks would completely change the nature of old-fashioned trench warfare. He didn't invent the name, though – the original prototypes were code-named 'Water Carrier' by the army. The military being the military, this was abbreviated to 'WC', but this was considered a bit too rude as WC also stands for water closet, or toilet – and who wants to be seen charging into battle in a Khazi? To save the soldiers' blushes, 'Water Carrier' became 'Tank' and the rest is history.

15 Fruit plays its part in modern car technology. The parcel shelf of the VW Fox is made from pineapples and the seats of the S-Class Mercedes are stuffed with a rare coconut husk, as are the wheel arches.

13 The first estate cars were called 'station wagons' and were vehicles designed for the sole purpose of taking your luggage from the train station to your hotel. They spread into the civilian world when people started to latch onto how useful they were.

14 The first Land Rover prototypes had the steering wheel in the middle. It's not exactly clear why – and not surprisingly, the idea was dropped by the time the production cars were built.

> **However competitive you are, resist the temptation to show you want to win... or you will look very sad.**

16 The first-ever car journey should by rights have been a monumental occasion with plenty of bunting and a mayor or two in evidence. In fact, this world-changing moment happened as a complete accident. Bertha Benz – wife of the inventor of the motor car, Carl Benz – borrowed her husband's machine in 1886 without telling anyone and drove it for sixty miles.

17 British Leyland was known for some staggering standards of workmanship, but the alleged Austin 1800 débâcle takes the biscuit. The car cost millions to develop but during the whole process none of the engineers clocked that the car they'd designed was two inches too wide to go through the tunnel from the assembly line to the paint shop.

18 The boot of the super-lightweight BMW M3 CSL is made of cardboard.

Mad
Motorsport
Moments

Focussed, determined and often quite bonkers, racing drivers are a rare breed. The lengths they will go to in order to win races, humillate their opponents, get girls and generally show off are something it's hard for the rest of us mere mortals to understand. One thing's for sure, whether winning, crashing or growing huge sideburns, racing drivers have provided us all with more than a century of entertainment. This is a small salute to some of their more outlandish antics.

It only takes a bit of luck...

Quite often a winning driver will publicly thank his team-mates, his mechanic, his manager and his sponsors as he takes to the podium. Frankly, it's a rather tedious spectacle and makes the whole thing look more like an Oscar acceptance speech by a Hollywood A-lister. It would have been fun, however, had Rubens Barrichello thanked the priest in a kilt who invaded the track at the 2003 British Grand Prix and effectively handed him the victory. The priest in question was 56-year-old Cornelius Horan, who leapt onto the circuit at the Hangar Straight, where the cars were doing almost 200 mph, to gain publicity for his religious views.

Ironically, Barrichello seems to have made a habit of winning races this way. He won his first Grand Prix at Hockenheim after a disgruntled Mercedes employee ran onto the track – some guys get all the luck.

It ain't what you do, it's the way that you do it...

The Bentley Boys, legendary playboy racers who made their name at Le Mans in the 1920s, certainly competed in style. As evening approached during the twenty-four-hour race, drivers would pull into the pits to change into formal black tie eveningwear before returning to the track to continue. One driver was even called in for an unscheduled pit stop and told, "The champagne is running out, sir – would you like the last glass?"

How did he do that?

In 1964, World Speed champ Craig Breedlove had a simply enormous crash in his Spirit Of America Land Speed Record Challenger. Driving at 539 mph across the famous Bonneville Salt Flats, his parachute failed to open – effectively, he had no brakes. He shot across a temporary wooden bridge at over 300 mph and somehow managed to steer through a line of telegraph poles before hitting a levee on the edge of a lake, still doing around 200 mph. The car took off, flew through the air and landed in the water. When the support crew arrived at the scene they expected to find their friend horribly mangled and dead. Instead Breedlove was standing on top of the half-sunken car, waving. "For my next trick," he shouted, "I'm going to set myself on fire."

If the van's a rockin'…

Most track marshals will tell you they have seen it all, but one of them certainly missed a crucial moment when legendary driver, playboy and hair-wearer James Hunt came to town. Hunt was competing in the Canadian Grand Prix and was enjoying some practice laps and pre-race testing the day before. The marshal in question had brought his girlfriend with him to watch – unwise really, rather like taking your rabbit to watch a greyhound race. In the event the young lady took as much of a shine to Hunt as he did to her – mind you, she was breathing – and made it clear that he was, to use the vernacular, 'in'.
He explained that if they were going to consummate their brief, but passionate relationship, their one chance to do so would be in the back of the circuit's ambulance – the one driven by her boyfriend. One of Hunt's many chums was called upon to distract the marshal while behind him, his ambulance rocked merrily on its wheels as Hunt managed yet another pole position.

Coming to a very full stop

In racing driver circles, they call it "going into the wall" and sometimes crashing is exactly that. But F1 driver David Purley took it to a new level when he hit the wall at a staggering 180 mph in 1977 while attempting to qualify for the British Grand Prix at Silverstone. As the wall was solid, his car stopped in just one metre, meaning he was subjected to an incredible 179g – the most even a modern F1 driver is likely to experience in a race without crashing is 5g – and they train all year round to be able to withstand it. Purley broke twenty-nine different bones, including his pelvis; he also dislocated three joints and suffered six heart stoppages. Incredibly, he survived the accident but sadly this popular racer, who won the George medal in 1974 for his attempted rescue of a fellow driver, was later killed when he crashed his Pittsburgh Special aerobatic plane in 1985.

Who said cheating was new?

Anyone complaining at a lack of sportsmanship in motor racing today would do well to look into the sport's history. An attempt to fix the 1933 Tripoli Grand Prix led to an on-track farce that could have ended the sport permanently. The Italian Government, desperate to build up the hype around the race, organised a lottery with millions of lira at stake. Enrico Rivio, a timber merchant from Pisa, drew a ticket bearing the name of driver Achille Varzi. Desperate to get his hands on the millions, he contacted Varzi and offered to split his winnings with him if he would fix the race. Obviously a man of dubious principles, Varzi went back to the rest of the drivers – similar men – made them an offer to split his share of the winnings and duly rigged the race.

On the day, though, Varzi had engine trouble at the very beginning with his car losing two cylinders and chugging along way behind the rest of the pack. From then on, the race deteriorated into a kind of cartoon, with the other drivers frantically trying to find convincing ways of losing to the trailing Varzi. One drove into some oil drums at a corner, another stopped with 'mechanical problems', while a third simply went into the pits and never came out. In the end just a driver called Nuvolari was left well in the lead with his car running beautifully. Now desperate for a way to throw the race and keep his dignity, Nuvolari pulled a stroke worthy of Basil Fawlty and simply coasted to a halt metres from the finishing line, claiming to have run out of fuel. His pit crew then performed a slow-motion re-fuel as Varzi spluttered past and won. Despite inquisitions and investigations, no action was taken apart from a decision to hold the lottery immediately before the start of the race in future.

Most
Amazing
Roads

Longest At 5,300 miles long, the Moscow to Vladivostock road dwarfs America's Legendary Route 66 (which stretches a mere 2,400 miles). Passing over the Ural Mountains, through the vast forests of central Siberia and along the Chinese border, the road has been discussed since the mid-sixties, but is only now nearing completion. The technical challenges are immense. Apart from the sheer length of the route – which passes through eight time zones – the road will have to cope with climatic conditions that are extreme, to say the least. Temperatures vary from 40°C to -50°C – try packing for your bank holiday trip on that one. Then there's the harsh and often mountainous terrain, which means over 250 bridges are needed. But there is a purpose to this mammoth project: many of the towns and cities along the way have only been within easy reach by train or air before, so this will provide a vital lifeline.

Shortest This is a short entry for a short street. Elgin Street in Bacup, Lancashire takes the title, being just 5 metres long. In fact, it's barely long enough to accommodate a family car, which makes it smaller than your average driveway.

Busiest The busiest stretch of road in the world is the 1.4-metre (0.9 mile) section of Los Angeles Freeway 405 known as the San Diego Highway, in Orange County. At peak times there's a traffic flow of 25,500 vehicles an hour. Now that can result in some pretty sticky traffic jams, but in fact the longest recorded jam occurred in France between Lyon and Paris in February 1980. Traffic headed towards Paris was backed up for a frightening 110 miles). Sacre bleu!

Wettest There can be only one winner in the wettest road category and it's the Bimini Road. For one thing, it's underwater, lying just off the island of Bimini in the Bahamas. Its claim to the soggy crown goes further even than this, however. Legend has it that the Bimini Road is the main highway leading to the lost city of Atlantis. It was first discovered in 1968, by a pilot who noticed the strange straight rock formations lying just 4.6 metres or so under the surface as he flew over the sea. On closer examination, the road turned out to consist of a series of rectangular stones laid out in two perfectly straight and parallel lines.

Coldest The coldest road in the world is the notorious Road of Bones, which sounds like something from *The Lord of the Rings*, but actually links the Russian cities of Magadan and Yakutsk in Siberia. The road is 1,250 miles long and was built in the Stalin era by political prisoners. Its forbidding name comes from the thousands of workers who died building the road. One of the towns on the road – Tomtor – is the coldest inhabited place on earth, with temperatures as low as -71.2°C.

Highest The Khardungla Pass in Kashmir, India holds the title as the highest road to be motored in the world, reaching a lofty 5,682 metres – more than four times the height of the very peak of Britain's highest mountain, Ben Nevis. At these altitudes, drivers will struggle with any physical exertion because of the oxygen-thin air. Changing a wheel on a car, for example, can take a seasoned mechanic nearly an hour rather than the ten minutes it would require at sea level. Even the cars themselves struggle: engines can't get enough oxygen and therefore can't burn as much fuel. At this height a typical engine will lose over 40 per cent of its power, which is a shame as the Khardungla Pass is not only the highest, but also one of the most hilly, roads in the world.

When Things Go Badly Wrong

The next time you stall at the lights, graze a gatepost or get pulled for your tax disc being a day overdue, don't run away seeking solace in a Kabbalah group: instead, try celebrating your shortcomings. The modern motorist's life is fraught with opportunities to make mistakes and cock-ups and generally look a plonker – it's what makes us human, or something. Below are some of the best examples in the world of how hopeless drivers can be. So, read them, memorise the stories and draw upon the experiences when the gear knob next comes off in your hand.

A driver in Stockholm was decapitated by a stop sign when he leaned out of a speeding car and yelled "Suckers!" at a pair of newly-weds posing for a photograph on the steps of a church.

Everything was going to plan for three prisoners escaping from a jail in Pretoria, South Africa... They clambered over the prison wall and ran to a parked car left by an accomplice. It was at that point that they discovered that none of them could drive. Now they are back in jail.

Lauren Rhoda performs a mind-reading act on the stage, but she's no superwoman. After claiming she had X-ray vision, she blindfolded herself and drove down a street in Ottawa, Canada. On the way, she hit three parked cars and a moving bus, and ended up in the front window of a store. She was then fined $6,000 with $79,000 damages, and banned from driving for life.

When he was stopped on a motorway, banned driver Piet Maas, 33, gave police in Rotterdam, Holland, a false identity – but they spotted his real name tattooed on his arm. He was arrested and later charged.

GERT MARITZ

In Brisbane, Australia, bungling crooks tried and failed to pull off the front of a cash point with their car. They left behind the bumper – complete with its number plate.

One irate young man in Florida, Orlando, was the driver involved in an accident. He wrote to his insurance company: "I was parked in lovers' lane with my girlfriend Alison. We were having a kiss and a cuddle and we got carried away with our emotions. I accidentally pushed the handbrake with my left foot as we made love and the car ran away down a slope and smashed into a tree. It was an awful shock for both Alison and myself, and especially for the peeping tom hiding behind the tree."

New York pedestrian Raymond Charman, 43, was lucky enough to escape unhurt from a car accident. However, his greed got the better of him and in an attempt to claim compensation, he lay down in front of the car. Unfortunately, it rolled forwards, crushing and killing him. He didn't get any compensation.

A hearse was in a collision in Milan, Italy. The body was thrown out of the coffin and the driver knocked unconscious. An ambulance arrived and the crew loaded the corpse into the ambulance – and the unconscious driver into the empty coffin. The mistake was only discovered at hospital when doctors found the body had been embalmed.

An ill-fated bank robber in Kansas, USA, put a mask on his face and drove up to a bank, leaving the engine running while he rushed into the building with a handgun. He tripped on a mat and, as he fell, the mask came off his face. He got up, bumped his head, fell over again and lost his gun. The staff and customers burst out laughing. He then fled out to his car only to find a policeman booking him for illegal parking, and is now in jail awaiting trial for armed robbery.

Police were called to a six-car pile-up – ten metres up in the treetops. The brand new Porsches were catapulted into a copse of trees when a transporter overturned near Bruchsal, Germany. Six of the eight cars on the transporter landed high in the branches and had to be rescued by a giant crane. A police spokesman said, "It was the first six-vehicle pile-up I've ever heard of with just one driver" – and, presumably, all in the same tree.

A sympathetic Belgian magistrate listened to tearful Mila Degrelle's story. It was her mother's illness, she claimed, that had caused her to momentarily lose concentration and back her car into another vehicle while out shopping the day before. Freed with a caution, Mila went into an Ostend bar for a celebratory meal. An hour later, coming out of the bar, she climbed into her battered Citroën and backed into the vehicle behind. The car belonged to the magistrate who had dealt with her case. Mila is now waiting to be presented at court again to meet a different, and perhaps sterner, magistrate.

Convinced he would go to hell when he died, Marc Baschet arranged for himself to be buried in a fireproof suit. The 57-year-old cancer victim from Lyon, France, was duly covered from head to toe in asbestos, and his steel coffin was also fitted with two fire extinguishers. And why was Baschet so sure he was destined for hell? Because of some of the bad things he'd done while working as a second-hand car salesman.

Arrested for drink-driving, Kurt Muller, 41, was also charged with vandalism after removing his artificial arm and using it to smash the windows of a police car in Berlin.

Wealthy cattleman Jake Fitte from Alberta, Canada, always mounts the heads of his favourite bulls on the cattleshed wall when they die. But a court has refused him permission to do the same with the head of his late wife Doris, who was killed in a car crash.

Armoured Cars

Armoured vehicles fascinate me. I hoard details on them in the same way that backwoodsmen in South Carolina collect the heads of hitchhikers. The modern machines of today, frequently used by diplomats and businessmen, usually add £100,000 to the price of the existing car but for that you get some formidable protection. Huge, thick slabs of armour-plated glass, for example, are now a bit last week. The new technology is one-way armoured glass, which stops bullets from coming in, but still allows the occupants to shoot out. Other protective devices include tyres that can run at nearly 60 mph after being shot out, Kevlar armoured body panels, an under-floor that can withstand a mine explosion and an internal oxygen supply that cuts in, should there be a poisonous gas attack. One grade higher into military hardware, the new Italian built replacement for the Army's Land Rover even has shock absorbers built into the occupants' seats so their bodies are cushioned from the blast of a landmine. These are defensive systems but if you want to hit back there are portholes, through which the occupants can fire guns and even Goldfinger-style gizmos for shooting out slippery oil jets at the rear.

Hitler's Armoured Car

Not one to leave his personal safety to chance, Hitler took to the streets in the Mercedes pictured below. It featured a 400-bhp motor (1), tyres with 20 cells to avoid shooting out (2), a windscreen of bullet-proof, 40mm-thick armoured glass (3), and general armour plating 18mm thick (13). The wings were made of aluminium for lightness (6), but carefully placed spare tyres (7) served as protective shields, and additional features included electro-magnetically operated doors (8), manganese-treated armour plating (9), and a petrol tank with a capacity of 300 litres (10). Hitler had this beauty fitted with a radiator of white copper (11) and his personal standard (12) for effect, asked for his seat (4) and footrest (5) to be raised by 13 cm each so that his admiring public could see him all the better, and then took to the streets with his head well clear of the top of the car. Amazingly, nobody took a shot.

And that brings me to a very important point: armoured cars only work if you're actually in them. When John Hinckley Junior tried to assassinate Ronald Reagan in 1981, the bullet that hit the President was one that had at first missed him, then bounced off the bodywork of his armoured limo straight into his body.

The First Presidential Armoured Car

A 1931 Cadillac that came into service in 1933 during the Roosevelt term of office was the very first US presidential armoured car. That's not interesting, but what is fascinating is the previous name in the car's logbook. The car in question had belonged to Al Capone. During the gun-happy days of the bootlegging Prohibition Era, he'd taken the initiative on armoured vehicles and when the Government seized Capone's assets on his arrest, the armoured limo made it to the White House.

Lawrence of Arabia

During battles with the Arabs for independence from the Turks, this legendary British freedom fighter depended heavily on his fleet of customised armoured Rolls-Royces. Throughout this campaign Lawrence was a busy man and his brand of guerrilla warfare – knocking out trains, bridges and platoons of troops in a single day – required transport that was both tough and fast for maximum mobility. He said his armoured rollers were worth 'above rubies' in the desert.

The Popemobile

Armoured vehicles usually have an air of menace about them – look at Hitler, for instance, in his armoured Mercedes. The protection vehicle with the least dignity about its person, however, must be the Popemobile. After the assassination attempt on Pope John Paul II in 1981, the poor guy was forced to lead the Catholic world from the back of this toughened ice-cream van. Not cool…

Weird Car Names

Every country has its own car culture, and these cultures all have their own little foibles. The French, for example, always take LSD before styling their cars; the British only like to start car ventures that are doomed to go out of business; and then we come to the Japanese... their party piece is naming cars.

Now giving a car a good name is important, and most manufacturers like to take their time over it. Ford spent almost a million pounds on marketing gurus in rectangular glasses before christening the Mondeo, and Volkswagen invariably take up months of boardroom meeting time analysing shortlists of contenders before choosing the word that will finally grace the rump of their next car. But the Japanese are much faster at getting to the point: they like to gather together a collection of random English words, shake them up in a Hoover bag, turn the nozzle from suck to blow, and then fire it at the back of the car in question. Whatever sticks is the name, as the examples on these pages will demonstrate.

The Life Dunk

The Delica Space Gear

The Grandis Chariot

The Rocky

The Bongo Friendee

The Big Thumb

Not all Japanese cars are named via the use of a game of Boggle and a Hoover bag. Some have much, much, much more science behind their application, as demonstrated by Nissan President Katsuji Kawamata. He gave the Nissan Laurel its name because he was a fan of Laurel and Hardy, and the Nissan Fairlady was so-called because he loved the musical *My Fair Lady*. Right.

Great car names are probably America's one decent contribution to the world. The Europeans, however, fail badly in this art. We always come over all pseudo techno and give everything letters and numbers: B200, 330d, C6, 575M, 911C4S, 207, A6... And when we do manage to dish out actual names, they're just a bit hopeless frankly. Look at the evidence: Marina, Princess, Golf, Vectra, Polo, Fiesta, Clio – they're the sort of names you give to fish that you win at the fair. Only Lamborghini – Diablo – and TVR – Sagaris, Tuscan – manage to salvage any European dignity at all. And then look at the Americans. Their cars may be completely wretched, but when they do bounce out of the factory with their jam-sponge suspension and K-Mart interiors, at least they go into battle with a good name. Scary animals is a common theme: Dodge Viper, Shelby Cobra, Pontiac Firebird, Plymouth Barracuda, Ford Mustang, Corvette Stingray, Cougar – all stuff that bites, stings, stampedes, or, in the case of the Firebird, is, erm, on fire, I think. In Britain if we went the animal route we'd probably go for the Ford Budgie, or the Vauxhall Gerbil. And when the Yanks have run out of animals, they just go for anything brash: Charger, Challenger, Prowler. And it works.

There is one area, however, where it doesn't matter which side of the pond you're on, all car makers are crap. And that's when they try to give their cars aspirational names to appeal to businessmen. You get words like "Executive" appearing on the boot – or worse, from Renault, the Renault 25 Manager. The Americans are just as bad. Take the Dodge Diplomat, the Ford Aspire or the Chevrolet Celebrity as evidence. Car companies are obsessed with business-men, but nobody else – you'll never see the Volkswagen Shop Assistant, or the Vauxhall Vet.

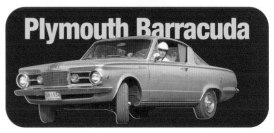

CAR NAME COCK UPS

Christening a car can cost around £1 million by the time you've hired the creatives in black polo necks, done the market research and carried out all the legal checks to make sure the name isn't already in use somewhere in the world. In spite of all that, though, things can still go wrong, in a Dennis Norden sort of way:

THE OPEL ASCONA This car sold well everywhere except in Galicia, the northwest region of Spain, where, amusingly, Ascona sounds like the word for a lady's private areas.

MITSUBISHI STARION This is the daddy of car name cock-ups. Mitsubishi already had a small car on sale called the Colt, and brought out a larger model that needed a name. The Japanese execs decided on the name Stallion, but when they informed the Australian Mitsubishi management of their decision, they did so over the phone... and the Australians faithfully wrote down the word "Starion". By the time the mistake was discovered, the badging and marketing campaign had begun and it was too late.

TOYOTA MR2 You wouldn't think you could go wrong with a combination of letters and numbers, but unfortunately for Toyota the French pronounciation "em er deux" sounds quite a lot like "merde" – or, in English, "shit".

BUICK LA CROSSE Nice work, except in Quebec, where LaCrosse is a slang term for masturbation. GM renamed the car in Canada.

FORD FIERA Spanish-speaking Latin Americans avoided this one, given that Fiera means "ugly old trout" in the local lingo.

MAZDA LAPUTA The Laputa had to be renamed in Spanish-speaking countries, where Puta means prostitute. With this in mind the ad campaign claiming that the Laputa "is designed to deliver maximum utility in a minimum space whilst providing a smooth comfortable ride" with its "impact absorbing body" probably didn't help that much either.

Richard Hammond's
Bedroom Wall Fantasies

Every year, manufacturers build cars so unbelievably gorgeous we'd all sell body parts to own them. They parade them in front of us, flaunt them until we're slobbering with lust and then throw them away, never to build another. These are the concept cars that only exist today as posters on my fantasy bedroom walls. In these pages, I have taken one car from each of the last six decades. It's probably best if you don't spend too long looking at these beauties: the inevitable disappointment could well lead to depression, despair and a life of crime and self-abuse.

Alfa BAT car

50s

No one had ever even heard of Batman when the first of the legendary Alfa 'BAT' cars appeared in 1953, so quite what they made of the super-futuristic shape of BAT 5, with its huge, curved fins, can only be imagined. The name came from Berlinetta Aerodinamica Tecnica. All three BAT cars were designed to be as slippery through the air as possible. The fins curved inwards, helping to control the airflow as it left the back, while openings in the nose allowed air to flow through the length of the car. In 1954, BAT 7 took the concept of aerodynamics even further, creating so little drag that its 1975 cc, 115 bhp Alfa Romeo engine could push it to 75 mph. It helped that the car was light, weighing only 998 kg – about the same as a modern-day Lotus Elise. BAT 9 was shown in 1955 and actually looked close to being a production reality, although it never was.

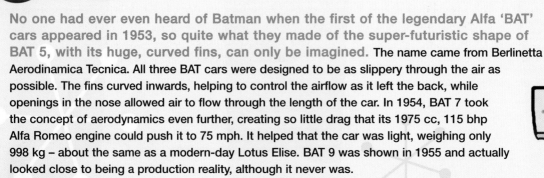

Lamborghini marzal

In the sixties people took a lot of drugs, but even so, the 1967 Lamborghini Marzal concept must have looked pretty far out. It had huge glass gull wing doors weighing so much that the body required masses of extra strengthening to cope. Designer Marcello Gandini (not a children's entertainer in his spare time, despite the name) was going through a bit of a hexagon phase, and his favourite six-sided shape made its appearance in the engine cover at the back, the shape of the front end, the dashboard and the centre console. The V12 from the Lamborghini Miura, then the company's real-life supercar, was too big so the designers cut one in half, making a 1965 cc, six-cylinder engine which they mounted towards the back of the Marzal. Perhaps not a rocketship in performance terms, but boy, did it create a stir visually.

Lancia Stratos

By the 1970s, people were so used to being 'spaced out' and flying to work on giant dandelions that it took a lot to shock them. So Lancia built the Stratos concept to remind them what "crazy man" really meant. At less than a metre high it could be driven out of the garage without opening the door. And actually, the car itself had no doors at all – there wasn't room for any in that super-low profile. Passengers would climb in through the windscreen, which opened upwards, probably with lots of dry-ice smoke pouring out and a noise like the door on the spaceship in *Close Encounters*. Visibility was poor, to say the least, but practicality wasn't really top of the list when this car was designed. The 1.6-litre V4 engine was taken from the Lancia Fulvia HF and lived under a triangular shaped panel at the back. The name Stratos was, of course, also given to the much later Lancia, er, Stratos.

Aston Martin
BULLDOG

With its straight lines and huge excesses in the engine department, the demurely named Aston Martin Bulldog couldn't be any more eighties if it rolled up its jacket sleeves and back-combed its hair. As if the massive 5.3-litre V8 wasn't enough, they added twin-turbos, which gave the Bulldog 650 bhp to play with. That meant it could hit 60 mph in 4.6 seconds and was officially verified as having done 192 mph. It was built as a showcase for the company's Tickford specialist engineering division. Typically for a concept car, they showed the world just what they could, and then didn't do it. Just one example was made, which sold for £130,000 in 1980.

AUDI AVUS

There's just one thing to say about the Audi Avus. Why isn't it built right now?

In 1991 Audi paraded the Avus in front of a drooling world and today it looks as tempting as it did back then. The technical specifications were the stuff of schoolboy dreams, too: a 6-litre, twelve-cylinder engine produced 509 bhp, which Audi claimed would send the Avus to 60 mph in just three seconds and on to a top speed of 211 mph. The engine's cylinders were in a 'W' formation, much like in the Bugatti Veyron of today.

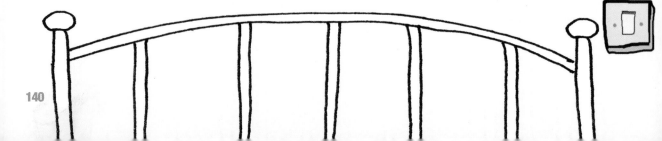

Maserati Birdcage

The name 'Birdcage' draws on Maserati's lengthy motor-racing heritage, being borrowed from the legendary Maserati Tipo 61 Birdcage race car built at the beginning of the 1960s. This stunning concept car was built in conjunction with Motorola, so perhaps we should be thankful it wasn't called the Maserati Flip phone.

Being a concept car of the 'noughties', the Birdcage's creators spend a lot of time going on about the 'fluidity of the technologies as a subsequent stage of the internet evolution' and how it is designed to have 'Maximum impact on the collective imagination' and make the 'Seamless Motibility vision real', rather than telling us how fast it goes. The good news is that underneath the gorgeous, flowing shape is the 6-litre V12 from the MC12, which shoves out 700 bhp, so speed will not be in short supply. The body was designed to be as aerodynamic as possible and special active aero panels at the rear can lift and move to alter the car's profile at speed, increasing downforce when it's required.

So-called because of its delicate and radical tubular chassis – which looked a bit like a birdcage only without the little mirror and the newspaper on the bottom – the original car of the 1960s featured large front screens which allowed a spectacular view of the car's mechanical workings. The huge area of glass on top of the 2005 Birdcage concept car is there for similar reasons; it isn't just to let passengers to see out, it's to let the rest of us peer in and admire the complex quadrilateral push-rod suspension and the carbon fibre inlet trumpets of the V12.

Picture Credits

The Orion Publishing Group has made every effort to contact and receive permission to use all the images contained in this book, and shall, if notified, correct any errors, oversights or omissions in subsequent editions.

Alamy 31, 131 (B), 136; Alfa Romeo UK 54-55; Alvey & Towers 17(main, BC), 19 (TL, BR); Andy Wilman Collection 83; Aston Martin UK 139; Audi UK 54 (T), 63 (R), 140; Bacup Council 122 (TL, BL); Blackhawk Automotive Museum, Danville, California, USA 27 (all images); BMW UK 114-115; British Motor Industry Heritage Trust 107, 114 (BL); Chris Shamwana 4, 32, 37, 46, 48; Citroën UK 64 (B); Corbis 22 (TR). 23 (T), 45 (R), 53 (BR), 58 (TL, BL), 67 (CL, CM, CR, BR), 93, 97 (both), 104 (B), 110 (TL), 120-121, 122 (TR), 123, 129 (T), 130 (all images), 131 (T); Daihatsu/IM Group 133 (TL); Daimler-Chrysler AG 54 (BL), 69 (all images), 114 (TR), 134 (BC); Doug Nye Collection 119 (BR); EMAP Autmotive/Max Power 25; Ford Motor Company 55 (T), 63 (BL), 72 (all images), 104 (T), 105 (BL); Gaydon 45 (CL); General Motors 64 (T), 134 (T, TC), 135 (TR, CL); Getty Images 23, 34-35, 38 (both), 47 (TL), 48 (R), 49 (L, R), 50 (both), 53 (BL), 91 (L), 109, 118 (BR); Goodyear Tyres 118 (TL, TR); Guinness World Records 88-89; Henry Ford Collection 110 (BL); Honda Racing 22 (BL); Imperial War Museum 10(R); Istockphoto 21 (main), 24 (TR); Jaguar Daimler Heritage Trust 113 (TR); Jeni Panhorst 113 (CL); Justin Hunt 47 (BR); 48 (BL) Lamborghini 53 (C), 77 (T, B), 137; Landrover UK 64-65, 65 (T); LAT Photographic 112 (TR), 119 (TL); Louwman Collection, Netherlands 28-29; Ludvigsen Library 73 (TR), 85 (T), 106 (both), 113 (BR); Mary Evans Picture Library 43, 76-77, 87, 129 (B); Mazda Motors UK Ltd 133 (TR), 135 (CR); Mitsubishsi Motors 132 (C, R); National Motor Museum, Beaulieu 42, 43 (T), 45 (TL), 81, 82, 102 (B), 111 (TR, BR), 112 (TL), 134 (C, B), 138; Nissan Motors GB 133 (C, BR); Pininfarina S.p.A, 141; Rex Features 17 (BL), 26 (T, B), 74-75, 78-79; Alisdair Macdonald 17 (BR); /David Hartley 58 (BR); /SIPA 59 (TR); /i2i 59 (C); /Everett Collection 110-111; /Keystone 114 (CL); Richard Hammond 2, 26 (both); The Harrah Collection, Reno, Nevada, USA 107 (B); The Tank Museum, Bovington 131 (C); Top Gear Magazine 67 (T), 102 (T, C); Toyota UK 135 (BR); Volkswagen UK 112 (BL, BR); Volvo Car UK 70-71; Walter P Chrysler Museum 101 (both), 105 (T); Weidenfeld & Nicolson Archives 6,9,10 (L), 16, 21 (TL), 24 (TL), 33, 36, 41, 51, 52, 61, 63 (both), 80, 88, 91 (R), 96, 100, 105 (BR), 108, 115, 120 (B), 124,1 25 (R), 128, 142; Wolseley Motors Ltd 103; www.mclellansautomotive.com 73 (B), 85 (B); www.thejackytouch.com 24 (BL, BC, BR);

Pages 98-99 all iStockphoto with the exeption of: 98 (r) DK Images, (t) Top Gear Magazine; 99 (c) Corbis, (l) Corbis, (o) Alamy, (p) Corbis, (t) Corbis

First published in Great Britain in 2006 by Weidenfeld & Nicolson
10 9 8 7 6 5 4 3 2 1

Copyright © text Richard Hammond & Andy Wilman 2006
Copyright © design and layout Weidenfeld & Nicolson 2006

All rights reserved. No part of this publication may be reproduced, stored
in a retrieval system, or transmitted, in any form or by any means, electronic,
mechanical, photocopying, recording or otherwise without the prior
permission of both the copyright owner and the above publisher.

The right of the copyright holders to be identified as the authors of this work has
been asserted in accordance with the Copyright, Designs and Patents Act, 1988.

A CIP catalogue record for this book is available from the British Library.

ISBN-13: 978 0 297 84445 7
ISBN-10: 0 297 84445 8

Design Direction by David Rowley
Designed by Ghost Design
In-house design team: Justin Hunt and Tony Chung
Picture and text research by John Lakey
Additional picture research by David Penrose
Cartoons by David Mostyn
Editorial by Debbie Woska

Colour reproduction by DL Repro, London
Printed and bound by Printer Trento srl

Weidenfeld & Nicolson
The Orion Publishing Group Ltd
Orion House
5 Upper St Martin's Lane
London WC2H 5EA

The Orion Group's policy is to use papers that are natural, renewable
and recyclable products and made from wood grown in sustainable forests.
The logging and manufacturing processes are expected to conform
to environmental regulations of the country of origin.